Eutychus (and his pin)

EUTYCHUS

(and his pin)

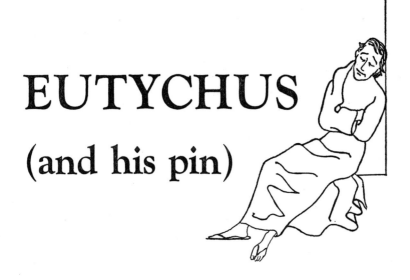

Edited, with an apology,
by Edmund P. Clowney

Wm. B. Eerdmans Publishing Company, Grand Rapids, Mich.

Printed in the United States of America

Introduction

Letters to the Editor are often a tale of woe, sometimes a pain in the neck (especially if it is migraine Monday), and now and then a lift to morale.

The anonymous feature signed EUTYCHUS has provided such crisp and rewarding reading in the first one hundred issues of *Christianity Today* that the best of these essays are herewith published in an anniversary folio. Simultaneously, the mystery of their authorship is ended, and we disclose their contributor to be the Reverend Edmund P. Clowney of Willow Grove, Pennsylvania, a gifted scribe whom I have known as such since the time when he edited the campus weekly, *The Wheaton Record.*

Through the years Ed Clowney has kept abreast of contemporary theological thought without loss of the biblical norm. Even now he is pursuing doctoral studies at Union Theological Seminary, New York. And as associate professor of practical theology at Westminster Theological Seminary, Philadelphia, he knows the practical dilemmas facing the modern minister within the church's situation in life.

Ever since his pithy items have appeared in *Christianity Today's* letter section, "Eutychus and His Kin," people have eagerly looked forward to Eutychus' next essay. One thing is sure: from the very first Eutychus has never been dull. Readers who may have missed this fortnightly funfest, with its subtle concern for higher and holier service in the cause of Christ, will profit from this unique blend of humor and Christian reflection.

—CARL F. H. HENRY

Editor, *Christianity Today*

On Behalf of Eutychus

It would be much beyond the competence of the author to present an adequate apology for this edition of pseudepigraphical literature. The bundle of letters which make up this book has been compiled from discarded copies of *Christianity Today*, in which the epistles of Eutychus and his kin are a perennial feature.

Eutychus was summoned to his post as a symbol of Christians nodding, if not on the window-sill, at least in the back pew. He has sought to prove, in this emergency, that the pin is mightier than the sword. His supreme accolade came from a fellow-correspondent who sent a genuine straight pin to use in deflating ecclesiastical pretense. Pin-wielding is a delicate art, however. Not everything that gets under one's skin is handled with the deftness of a hypodermic needle, and the effect is sometimes anything but therapeutic. In this selection, some of the more heavy-handed pin jabs have been dropped; the others, it is hoped, are at least cushioned.

This is the proper occasion for warm appreciation to the many kin of Eutychus who have responded in letters often illuminating and sometimes illuminated, with the gilding of a medieval manuscript. Among these treasures is a superb translation of Ecclesian into Pennsylvania Dutch. None, however, are more rewarding than the red-faced replies of those who wrote to Hybrid, Nebraska, for the *Kirkit* (see page 100).

There are hazards in withdrawing from the aloofness of pseudonymity. May I plead that the shelter was designed as a cloister and not a duck-blind! Since drowsiness in my case is in no sense fictional, perhaps I may hang up a "Do Not Disturb!" sign, and retreat to my window seat. The first epistle of Eutychus, which follows, will serve to introduce the name, and this collection.

— EDMUND P. CLOWNEY

On Eutychus

This hasty note is past my deadline because I fell asleep while composing a letter of congratulation to the editor of *Christianity Today* on the beginning of another year of publication. I was reassured to read recently that chronic sleepiness can be inherited. Perhaps I share a congenital affliction with my ancient namesake at Troas.

May I suggest a study of the original Eutychus? Preachers, at least, should know how to spell and pronounce his name (Yew′-ti-cuss—ED.). The name meant "good luck" in an age when Lady Luck was even more fervently worshiped than at our race tracks.

Do you suppose anyone reflected on the name when Paul's prolonged discourse was interrupted by the abrupt disappearance of "Lucky" from the window sill? Was anyone shaken by a sudden thought that the goddess Tyche was revenged on an apostate from an old cult?

At any rate, the First Church of Troas, without the benefit of centuries of jokes about sleeping in church, no doubt failed to see anything comical in the still form on the dark street. Yet their joy must have been the richer when Eutychus was restored. The gates of death could not prevail against the church of Christ. The bondage of "good luck" was broken by the Good News.

Too many Christians still live with crossed fingers, sweating out their good luck as a portent of calamity. To see them you would never guess that God's good pleasure and not the goddess of Fate rules human destiny.

No doubt Eutychus should have been listening and praying rather than sleeping, but childlike faith and deep sleep are not unconnected. Tyche's devotees are great insomniacs; they must keep one eye on their capricious goddess. The psalmist, on the other hand, said, "In peace will I both lay me down and sleep" for the Lord who never slumbers was his Keeper.

At least Eutychus didn't need a sleeping pill.

—EUTYCHUS

7

Contents

Introduction   5

On Behalf of Eutychus   6

On Eutychus   7

FROM THE WINDOW SEAT

Isaac   15

Ta Thung   16

Big and Little   17

Tourists and Pilgrims   18

The Added Ingredient   19

Through the Looking-Glass   20

Big Smoke   21

Remember   22

Cartoon of the Month   23

Bedtime Story   24

Communication   25

Galbus in Perpetuum   26

M. G.   27

The Sin of Flesh   28
Favorite Greeting   29
To H. W. L.   30
Introspection   31
The Man with the Book   33
Championship Play   34
Old Grad   35
Census   36
Hypertension   37
Fashion Guide   39

CUTTING THE CLOTH

Pastoral Problem   43
Pastoral Problem II   44
Comparative Ecclesiastics   45
Pastor's Sermon Clinic   46
Collage   47
Minister Cheevy   49
Sacred Electronics   50
Sermon Doodles   51
Preacher's Mathematics   53
In and Out the Windows   55
Fellowship Quilt   56
Sound the Trumpets   57
Spectators   58

MARKING TIMES

Halloween Reformation   61
Reformation Day   62

Saints and Spooks 63
Thanksgiving Farce 64
13 Shopping Days 65
Santa Forum 66
Mirth at Christmas 67
New Year Bells 68
Valentine Bouquet 69
All Out for Easter 71
Flies or Ants? 73
The Freedman 74
Spending Vacation? 75

TEACHER'S RETREAT

Limericks for Sunday School 79
Rally Day Acrostic 80
Zoo, Please! 81
Self-Service School? 83
Have Fun! 84
The E-Bomb 85
The Child and the Children 86

ECCLESIAN MADE EASY

Lesson I 91
Verdict in Ecclesian 92
Humpty-Dumpty 93
Key to Ecclesian 94

ON THE SHELF

Book of the Fortnight 99
Summer Sleuths 101

From the Window Seat

Isaac

Is humor worldly and unchristian? The Preacher "said of laughter, It is mad; and of mirth, What doeth it?" There are not many jokes in the Bible. A merry heart may be good medicine, as psychosomatic therapists continue to assure us; but after a sober look at our human predicament we may turn to a double dose of drugs instead.

The sneers, snickers, giggles, guffaws, and belly laughs we hear about us are not reassuring. Laughter seems lewd, or mocking, or hollow — more hellish than heavenly. We hear echoes of the jeering on Golgotha. Shrill laughter, taut with fear and hatred, greeted the jokes at the foot of the Cross. They ridiculed the absurdity of this man who made himself equal with God, this crucified Messiah.

Yet they were the fools. In the irony of divine judgment their wicked jests preached the Gospel: "He saved others; himself he cannot save!" These rulers who set themselves against the Lord's Anointed became the objects of the dreadful laughter of God's derision. Satan became a laughingstock at Calvary, for his triumph there was his destruction.

Ever since that moment the foolishness of the Cross has been the power of God to salvation. Men still laugh at the Cross and scoff at "butcher shop theology," but heaven's laugh is last.

The irony of sin's complete frustration, dark with God's wrath, is not heaven's greatest triumph over sinful folly. There is also the ineffable humor of grace; the joy in heaven over one sinner who repents. Here is unimaginable absurdity; mighty angels are hilarious because old John Smith is crying. All of grace is like that — incongruous, unthinkable, amazing. The son of the promise is Isaac — laughter! Abraham laughed that he should be a father; Sarah laughed that she should bear a son — how absurd! And when he

15

was born, she found a new laughter: "God has made me to laugh; everyone that hears will laugh with me."

The joy we share with Sarah, and the virgin Mary, and Mary Magdalene may be more than laughter, but it is not less. So marvelous is the wonder of His redemption that our old sorrows seem ludicrous, as ludicrous as Mary's weeping before the empty tomb and taking the risen Lord for a gardener!

It is amusing to think of a camel's going through the eye of a needle; but it is divine comedy indeed, amazing, laughable, wonderful — to be a redeemed sinner entering heaven's feast!

Ta Thung

I have just returned from the beach. It is such a relief to get away from the city crowds on the street and get among the city crowds at the shore. I love to watch the ocean. Since I couldn't see it for people, I decided to watch people. Ocean watchers, prone on the sand, can observe the bubble and wash of spent waves, the boisterous dance of the junior combers, and beyond, in endless line, the proud plunging plumes of the great breakers. People watchers, from a similar posture, can observe padding feet, mincing legs, peeling haunches, paunches, sagging silhouettes, and the endless line of beach umbrellas — until a rush of running feet ends all vision in a blinding sandstorm.

The charm of the beach is equaled only by the subway in achieving the modern ideal of "togetherness." Even the Iron Curtain is no screen against togetherness. The Chinese Communists call it *Ta Thung*, "the Great Togetherness," a phrase from the classics describing a legendary golden age. *Ta Thung* can also mean "great similarity," a remarkably apt term for the drab, mechanized uniformity of totalitarian togetherness. Seaside togetherness is not mechanized or drab, but just as uniform, in spite of the best efforts of swimsuit stylists.

Too often togetherness is confused with the Christian ideal. The notion of heaven which masses lounging saints on a golden strand can be forbidding to a man fresh from the seashore. Dante saw unending proximity as one of the torments of hell.

16

What makes comradeship a delight, and a great host inspiring? Not that they are together, but what they share together. Christian fellowship is *koinonia,* a sharing in the blessings of God. Christians are together with one another because they are together with Christ.

Without this relation to the Giver and Meaning of life, togetherness is only crowded emptiness. Men surrender their personal freedom to the packed prisons of mass society and the modern state in vain flight from loneliness — and God. We find one another when we are found of Him, and join the singing saints in the Ta Thung in Christ.

Big and Little

Ever since skyscrapers began to pile up in New York, bigger and better have been synonyms for bigtime advertising. Giant, colossal, king-sized, mammoth products fill our supermarkets. In the buildup only these words have been cut down. When the man in the ad declares, "I like my pleasures *big!*" he seems to mean that he prefers large parties, big yachts, and huge trailers, and a cigarette about a half inch longer.

The Brobdingnagian trend is clear enough, however, to anyone who tries to fit a giant box of cereal on a kitchen shelf or a new car into the garage. The motorist who surveys hundreds of long, *long* automobiles jammed bumper to bumper on a superhighway like dinosaurs in a mudhole may even speculate on the fate of Henry Ford's thunderlizard.

The answer of course is miniaturization. Lilliputians and transistors are providing us with pocket radios, wrist cameras and scooter cars. The transition may be uncomfortable as we crawl into knee-high racers, but our products come in two sizes only: midget and mammoth. In religion, too, Americans like superlative extremes — miniature chapels or towering cathedrals. One of the problems facing mass evangelism is its fascination for people who like their religion big — and find a church of average size with a preacher of ordinary gifts altogether uninspiring. Our universe is a harmony of atoms and galaxies, but we are not made to live on either scale. Two or three Christians may know the Lord's presence even as a stadium rally may taste His blessing, but neither group is a normal size for a functioning Christian congregation.

Many Americans crave a big church because their God is too small. The superlatives of the Gospel are things which are not seen, and eternal. For our daily Christian life and work we need the family size.

Tourists and Pilgrims

All men are strangers and travelers. Our fathers were pilgrims; we are tourists. The difference is more vast than the breadth of the continent spanned by generations of pioneers. The tourist, to be sure, sees a distinction. It adds relish to his feeling of superiority as he squeals around the curves of some historic trail in the foothills of the Rockies. An unusual and imaginative tourist may even speculate, while picking his teeth in an air-conditoned "chuckwagon," as to how his day's drive compares with the best performance of a Connestoga "schooner."

Yet the fondness of tourists for playing at being pioneers suggests a difference of another order, one that cannot be measured by the horsepower superiority of the high compression engine.

The pilgrims traveled with purpose. Between decks in the crowded little *Mayflower* was a seriousness that our generation can only imitate in the convulsive hysteria of war.

Lack of seriousness is the tourist's mark. Flipping wisecracks and cigarette butts, he squanders money to pass time. The wonders of an electronic age provide him with gambling devices in the majesty of the desert and comic books on the mountain top. His use of leisure projects in three dimensions the emptiness of his heart.

Every pilgrim seeks a city, a country, a home. The tourist is only leaving his home, or rather losing his home in aimless compulsive wandering. It was not the disappearance of the American frontier that made his travels pointless. Nor will new frontiers on Mars help him. He seeks no frontier, for he has lost himself. In his vacuum of faith he needs to hear the call to the heavenly city; to become a pilgrim; to go out — and come home!

18

The Added Ingredient

While brushing my teeth this morning I noticed that the family toothpaste was in a bright new tube. Another miracle ingredient, Amalgam-58, has been added. Without my glasses, I couldn't make out what magical properties the additive possesses. Judging from the plastic adhesiveness of a ribbon of the stuff that had squirted along the wall, I would surmise that Amalgam-58 not only fights decay for 58 hours but also fills cavities.

I sighed contentedly through the foam. The bubbles that drifted off reminded me of the detergent action that had been added a year ago. Before that it had been FL-7, ammoniate, and chlorophyl.

And before that? Years of faithful brushing with plain, unfortified, non-miraculous, ordinary toothpaste, a mere medium for FL-7 and Amalgam-58. It is the additive that counts in any product, as the TV laboratory demonstration invariably proves. "In this beaker we have ordinary eyewash . . ." Already we view it with contempt. Colorless, insipid, ordinary eyewash that could scarcely float a beam out of a brother's eye if applied with a fire-hose. But sparkling in the other beaker is eyewash with *retinium*. Even before the glass eyeball is dropped in, we know that this is the deep-acting ingredient that will penetrate to every rod and cone of the retina.

Madison Avenue agencies have at last convinced us that man does not live by bread alone, but by the added ingredients.

Only as bold a writer as C. S. Lewis would entitle a book *Mere Christianity*. Leaders of the flourishing isms are all advertising what has been added. The golden tablets dropped from heaven at Palmyra, N. Y., make all the difference. More refined revisions of Christianity have a similar zeal for the insights of some leaders of neo-theological fashion.

Even stout defenders of plain Christianity are not immune to the lure of the added ingredient, as compounded perhaps by a sensational Bible teacher. Worst of all, sometimes the Gospel itself is promoted as something added, a booster shot of happiness, instead of a new life in Christ Jesus. God's saving power operates not by addition, but by transformation.

Through the Looking-Glass

In Philadelphia a police magistrate sobers up his daily haul of drunks with a big mirror on the station house wall. They don't like what they see, and most of them are ready to take the pledge after one good look. If this mirror trick works, we can expect most of our metropolitan station houses to be renovated along the lines of the Hall of Mirrors at Versailles. Anything to cut down on the hordes of smashed, schnoggered inebriates who clutter the magistrate's blotter — more than 10,000 this year in the station which now has the mirror!

No doubt we will soon have some psychological studies on mirror therapy. Perhaps the psychoanalyst's couch might be equipped with a mirror on the ceiling. Short of Cinemascope, there is nothing like a mirror to see yourself as others see you.

There seems to be one difficulty, however. Long before the station house had a mirror, most of the bars were lined with them. Somehow the mirror seems to work better when a hangover has made a man more reflective. The behavior of certain Hollywood citizens who have a maximum installation of bedroom mirrors suggests that plate glass alone is not the answer. If Narcissus had been furnished with modern mirrors he might have perished of self-love on the spot. The daily mirror reveals one's least secret admirer.

There has been one substantial improvement on mirrors for spiritual therapy. The women who ministered at the door of the tent of meeting brought their brass mirrors to Moses, and he cast them into a laver, according to the pattern he received in the Mount. A mirror never flatters; a morning-after mirror may bring the truth of despair. But only a laver cleanses.

James exhorts us to look into the mirror of the Word, not as idle spectators, toying with a vanity glass, but as doers, obedient to the law of liberty. There is one mirror where a man may see himself as God sees him. The shock is greater than at the mirror in the station house. But God's mirror is a laver where his sin is cleansed and where the reflected image at last is like Christ.

Big Smoke

Americans spend 3 billion annually for their churches and 6 billion for cigarettes. To the cigarette industry it may seem that the churches have done well, considering their modest advertising budget and extremely soft sell.

Suppose Madison Avenue were to be given some ecclesiastical accounts. Imagine national magazines featuring color cover ads with a rugged fullback emerging from church: *Join the men who know; get that big clean feeling!*

Or perhaps in the church news column we might read, "First Church has reduced theological irritants to the lowest level among all leading pulpits. First Church preaching is smooth. It's First for filtered truth!"

Television spots could feature the new preacher in his pulpit at Central Church: *It's what's up front that counts!* Such proven slogans as *There's no substitute for quality!* would need no revision. The spring freshness theme would be another natural; it should apply to religion almost as well as to tobacco.

The super-science of the cigarette ads might be harder to adapt. "Important break-through in biblical research. Get that extra Dead Sea flavor in every sermon." Church architecture suggests other scientific areas: "High porosity in our acoustical vault air-softens every choir note."

The better the makin's, the better the sermon. This could caption an oil painting of a craggy-browed clergyman among his books. Of course he would have his sleeves rolled up to show an anchor tattoo. "If you're thinking of changing churches, tattoo this in your mind. . . . Deepwell's exclusive preaching formula gives you religion you can get hold of."

The competitive claim might not prove attractive to church advertisers. A new campaign could be developed: "Remember, the brand makes no difference! Wherever church bells ring you get the real thing."

Is this sufficiently absurd? We have almost stopped laughing at those serious cigarette ads; when we do, we are not far from the king-sized pitch in religion — enjoyed in all the 50 states!

Remember

The memory course I am taking will soon make me the envy of Cloverleaf Vista. Already I have mastered my telephone number, my car license, and Lincoln's Gettysburg address. No longer will I have to stage violent coughing fits on those dismal occasions when I stand between two life-long acquaintances who have not been introduced. Names will pop up like toast at fellowship breakfasts, alumni dinners, and business luncheons.

I know it will work this time, because the course was written by a psychologist who won fame on a quiz show through sheer concentration and association. After all, it doesn't help to get the answers in advance if you can't remember them in front of the camera.

There are still a few wrinkles to be ironed out. It was disconcerting to greet Dr. Pike so warmly as Bill Mackerel. Understandably, the proper fish slipped off my memory hook, but the switch from Doctor to Bill was more disturbing. Unfortunately, I had visualized a pill to associate Pike with his profession. However, the course has three more days to go and by then I should be ready to develop applied mnemonics for pastors. If your minister can't remember your name at the church door, and has forgotten the date of the Sunday School picnic, just send his name to me.

I have already approached Pastor Peterson on the subject. He has agreed to try it out if it works for me.

He says that memory is very important in the Bible, but the scriptural emphasis has more in common with Memorial Day than with memory systems. God remembers his people in his covenant faithfulness and calls on them to remember him. The aids to memory in the Bible are the memorials of God's promises, among them the rainbow and God's own memorial Name. Scripture itself is a memorial record of God's purposes, a book of remembrance pointing to Christ. In the Lord's Supper the death of the Saviour is commemorated in our memorial feast.

There was much more that the pastor said, but I don't remember it all. It was so fascinating I almost forgot why I had come.

Cartoon of the Month

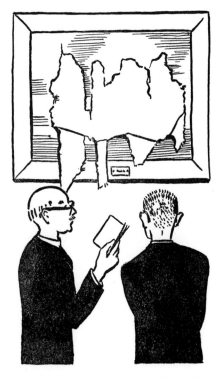

It says, "The picture plane is broken through to recover the lost dimension of depth."

CARTOON EXPLANATION:

The two clergymen in the picture are in an art gallery. One is reading from a guidebook. The masterpiece they are inspecting has felt the impact of a recent article by a Harvard theologian. The professor says that the dimension of depth is religious. He seems to feel that modern art has it all over Billy Graham in this dimension. It asks a sincere and religious question "when the painter breaks the visible surface into pieces."

This picture shows how sincere a painter can get.

It also *symbolizes* what I think the professor has done to the Christian gospel in seeking his lost dimension of depth.

23

Bedtime Story

The last bedtime story I read to my youngest daughter has been keeping me awake. There are no giants, witches, or dragons in it. Nancy and I are both old-fashioned, and neither loses sleep over fee, fie, fo, fum.

This story is most contemporary. It is about a dog named Crispin's Crispian, who belonged to himself, and therefore kept house with bachelor methodicalness. After a few curious adventures, he met a boy who also belonged to himself. On the dog's invitation, the boy came to share his house.

Share is not exactly the word, since each of these rugged individuals emphatically preserved his own independent way of life. On opposite pages each chewed up his own dinner and swallowed it into his stomach. Then, also on opposite pages, each went to bed and dreamed his own dreams.

The disturbing thing is that I don't know what to make of this philosophical novel for the kindergarten. It is just as evident that I should understand it. There could hardly be more clues. The dog, for example, takes himself for a walk. He can go wherever he wants, but he doesn't know where he wants to go.

This would seem to be the dilemma of the freedom of modern man. The emancipated individualist, without restriction, is also without goals or norms. The man who belongs to nobody has nowhere to go.

Crispian's solution, in advice that he gives himself, is just to walk; sooner or later he will get somewhere. I take it that he is no existentialist. The advice smacks more of Dewey than Sartre. Or perhaps it is just the spirit of the frontier.

From this point on I become more confused. The walk takes Crispian to a dog country and a cat and rabbit country with implications that are either political or Freudian, and then the dog-meets-boy theme develops.

There is an outright declaration that the dog is a conservative, who likes everything in place, whether saucers or stars. Yet I am not reassured. The domiciled coexistence of this dog without a master and boy without a father seems to be a dreadful parable of society without God, where there can be fraternization but not fellowship, cooperation but not love.

I do wish the author were at least less profound, for the sake of the parents, who also need their sleep. How about a little lost puppy who comes home to his master? At bedtime.

Communication

After an historic title bout someone asked Sugar Ray Robinson how far the knockout punch had traveled. "I don't know," answered the champion middleweight, "but he got the message somewhere!" The crack is not so classic as Sugar Ray's left hook, but it has a future. It is made to order for all these talks about talking and should appear in dozens of commencement addresses.

Sugar Ray was using the language of a communication-conscious age. Since our society is being reshaped by electronic means of communication, we cannot avoid the subject. With curious zeal, many people want to reduce everything to communication. Skeptics assure us that we have outgrown all talk about what *is*, and that we must be satisfied with the logical analysis of how we used to talk about it. T.V. surely demonstrates how much more we know about *how* than *what* to communicate!

The old liberalism believed that education would solve all problems. Today's liberal has the same naive faith in communication. Communicate in print, at the conference table, or on the psychiatrist's couch, and conflicts will evaporate. The trouble is that the message, on delivery, is often a left hook to the chin!

Some preachers are far more ready to discuss communication than the Gospel to be communicated. The difference between heaven and hell becomes an exercise in semantics. By separating language from truth, men justify using expressions they no longer believe and at the same time deny that God can reveal his truth in human language.

Those who believe that God's Word is truth need a new grip on "communication" — and revelation. But they must avoid the method of the wise man of Gotham, who decided he needed a better grip while hanging from a tree branch over the sea, and therefore let go to spit on his hands.

Galbus in Perpetuum

Time quotes this profound observation by a reflective British bureaucrat: "Progress depends on whether there is a red light or a green light. What is important is that the lights should not be set forever at amber."

The remark assumes a British respect for law, and would not be intelligible to the hot-rodder to whom yellow only signals a burst of speed. Properly understood, however, this contemporary *logion* could provide our chief ecclesiastical motto. I have approached a church goods manufacturer about issuing a blinker lamp for committee rooms with an etched inscription, "Forever Amber." (He suggested that for church use it might be better to Latinize the phrase; I think it was *Galbus in Perpetuum.*)

Committees are essential to our society as centers of indecision. The allegation that a camel is a horse put together by a committee is a manifest fabrication, since no committee could formulate anything less compromising than a swoose.

Unhappily, Christianity is often understood as the religion of committeemen. Caution, mediation, and compromise are made the Christian virtues. To the amber-minded, it is most unchristian to say that anybody or anything is wrong. No final attitude should be expressed on any question from communism to church carpeting. Everything is fluid in the ongoing conversation on all subjects. But the fluid has the highest viscosity, and nothing goes on with any speed.

Sometimes a red or green light shines from the pulpit, but usually the amber is timidly blinking. The preacher is neither modernist nor fundamentalist, but is dialectically hovering somewhere between a conservative liberal and a liberal conservative. Following the amber gleam, the church can move toward the sublime uncertainties of better adjustment.

The Gospel was not arrived at in committee, and the prophets denounce those who halt between two opinions. Christ detests lukewarm disciples. To be hot or cold is better, individually or in committee. Even a committee can seek first the Kingdom, instead of a working formula.

26

M. G.

According to our newsmagazine, Good Guys and Bad Guys are part of a TV myth that is disappearing. Soon existential man will be in the saddle. He shares in a larger identity of Good and Evil, and is neither hero nor villain. He is more than a myth, a Free Man. As I remember Olympus, the myths were not too strong on pure types of Good and Evil. However, modern thinkers are ready to make the mythical purely good if that will serve to make the purely good mythical.

Western writers may need help in building up this mixed hero/villain to the point where kids will buy his autographed cap pistols. Perhaps he should be introduced on a few programs along with the standard Good Guy and Bad Guy as the M.G. (Mixed, Muddled, or Modern Guy).

Scenario for M.G.

B.G. These knots is tight. You won't get out of this. Light the fuse, M.G.!

G.G. (Gagged) Awg...ahlwahch!

M.G. Why don't you tie me up too?

B.G. Like to oblige, but I need ya on my next job, M.G. Light the dynamite!

G.G. (Still gagged) *See above.*

M.G. You're a dynamic man, B.G., but are you as free as you think? Why must you kill? You're punishing yourself!

B.G. You got it wrong, kid. *You're* the dynamite man in this outfit. And I ain't killin' G.G. You are. Light the fuse or I'll ventilate ya.

M.G. Certainly. I was just looking for a match. You know I'm your partner. But couldn't we take the gag out? No one will hear him in this abandoned mine. Besides, your mortido urge...

B.G. Okay, okay. Take out the gag. Here, give it t' me. Now let me bung that big mouth of yours. There. Now light that fuse!

G.G. While that fuse burns, B.G., I want to say I never knew you salted the mine.

B.G. Why then...M.G., you rat...I *will* lace you up too, pardner! Gotta hurry. Keep still, or I'll...WHOOM! BOOOM! (etc.)

G.G. That was a break. I must have been blown clear up the air shaft.

B.G. (Muffled) Help!

G.G. You too! Here, I'll drop this rope down to you. Where's M.G.?

B.G. He's done for. All mixed up, kinda.

G.G. Maybe it's better that way. C'mon, hombre, I'm takin' you to the sheriff.

The Sin of Flesh

No suburbanite could make the Manichean mistake. The American body is not evil! Indeed, there is only one sin of the flesh likely to arouse modern guilt feelings: the sin of the bulge. How the Psalmist could envy those whose eyes stood out with fatness is now hard to imagine. Ehud's treatment of the king of Moab seems more understandable; what else can a fat man expect?

This widespread anxiety feels the pinch each spring, for last summer's wardrobe — in fact, any summer wardrobe — demands a more fashionable shape.

In the days when other fleshly sins were taken seriously, fasting and spiritual exercises were zealously practiced. Contemporary saints of physical culture urge similarly drastic remedies. They rally the faithful with magazine homilies on eight-day diets. Photographs of their graceful deep-knee bends guide the struggles of those with less bounce and more ounces.

Such measures are for the stern. Others prefer the Ramadan plan: fast in the day and feast at night. But the ideal weight-lifting scheme requires no exertion, permits gorging as usual, and gives astounding results in 10 days. It is, of course, a blend of chemistry and electronics. One smokes reducing cigarettes and eats reducing candy while relaxing the pounds away in a contour massage chair. To repeat the achievement, shut off the current and put the weight on again in the same chair!

With such electronic control of the flesh, guilt becomes nominal. Remaining tensions may be eased by a taste of religious TV, or dissipated on the new plug-in psychosomatic couch, where the soma is vibrated while the psyche is analyzed. Even the mortido drive is satisfied as one settles back in his own electric chair. The placidity of vibratory sedation is just this side of Nirvana.

28

Favorite Greeting

If Nancy had not fallen into the Christmas tree, I might never have noticed. I was quietly reading a back number of *Time* (when I recover my copy from the boys' wastebasket or under the *All* in the laundry, it is always a back number); I was reading, I say, *Time* (and don't think there is any payola in my plugging that magazine or mentioning a detergent; sometimes I wish I were not so anonymous).

I'll begin again. I was quietly reading when Nancy fell into the Christmas tree. It was a routine holiday accident. Nancy, age four, was crying because she couldn't touch the star on the top of the tree, and Willie was lifting her up so that she could, and Charles was lying on the floor watching television, and Sue was practicing a dribble and lay-up shot with an imaginary basketball. Sue stumbled over Charles and clipped Willie, who windmilled wildly before catapulting Nancy into the middle of the tree. The whole incident didn't take more than five seconds, and everything was set right in two or three hours, including replacing the tree lights and getting three stitches in Nancy's chin.

However, I recalled, while I was searching for the magazine again, that I had been reading about the success of Mr. Hall of Hallmark Cards (remember, I don't receive even a complimentary get-well assortment out of this). I had just come to the sentence that stated what the alltime best selling card was when the catastrophe struck. What was that alltime bestseller? The question became important. Here was an image of an age. This is the kind of thing a budding sociologist takes seriously. No doubt the bestseller would be seasonal. Perhaps a wise men design, symbolizing the yearning of modern man for his dimly remembered faith.

Three days later, I found the right magazine in the public library. I finished the article. The alltime bestselling card shows a cart loaded with pansies.

I walked home through the sleet. Am I, too, a beatnik at heart? What's wrong with pansies? Perhaps they will become the national flower. Or does this account for the "time wounds all heels" variety of cards that are now taking over at the drug store? Is this the revolt of existentialism against the old liberal optimism of the pansies? Does the elderly Mr. Hall have the same sure touch in selecting designs for these weirdies?

There was a get-well greeting for Nancy in the mailbox from Aunt Sally. Yes, a cartload of pansies.

To H. W. L.

Lives of great men all remind us
Maladjustment is sublime;
Non-conforming leaves behind us
Footprints on the sands of time.

Tracks that spurn conditioned masses,
Crowding in canalized grooves,
Mark the pioneer who passes
Beaten paths the group approves.

Let us, then, be up and doing,
Deviate our attitudes,
Rock our social role, pursuing
Our abnormal aptitudes!

Life is real! Life is earnest!
And the mean is not the goal;
Normal curves are not the sternest
Mark and measure of the soul!

If computer correlation
Lacks percentiles for your case,
Just employ your situation
To observe the human race.

Every function, status, mission
Can be socially defined
Just because the statistician
Never had your id in mind.

Since an average distribution
Rates performances by par,
You may rate an institution
With a profile so bizarre!

If your size would shame Colossus
Group dynamics in a week
Offers, through adjustment process,
Your acceptance — as a freak!

Do you differ in your fears?
Whiskers? I.Q.? Art? or ears?
Please remember that your peers
Have one catalogue for queers.

Go your way in isolation,
Carrying "Excelsior,"
Shunning every explanation
As to what it's useful for.

But remember, footprint maker,
You may soon expect to find
As you cross some upland acre,
Power shovels close behind!

Introspection

I love my problems, hold them tight,
And I enjoy them every night:
Two hundred of them, all acute,
And every one of them a beaut!
Through expert agonized reflection
I have selected my collection;
They all are free of imperfection.
All are hopelessly involved;
None can possibly be solved.

31

For those that I have most enjoyed
I owe a debt to Sigmund Freud;
It's hard to beat the bitter bliss
Of utter self-analysis.

No analyst at any fee
Could find more ambiguity
In conflicts that I have with me,
Or show permissive empathy
To such astonishing degree
As I can, existentially.
(Especially from one to three —
The wee small hours seem to be
Most suited psychologically
To contemplate my quandary.)

I love my problems, and resist
Suggestions that they don't exist.
Of course their structure so refined
Projects the warped woof of my mind
(For my repression never hid
The shape of my eccentric id),
And I would never take the view
That these concerns exist for you.

They are my problems, is that clear?
Please curb your wish to interfere.
Remove my problems that I might
Go back to counting sheep at night?
Now, if I were to share with you
A little glimpse of one or two . . .
You would be quick to take my view:
For though you could persuade me to
Accept the universe as such
My self-acceptance is too much!

The Man with the Book

Now I saw in my dream, as Christian went on his way toward the city, reading from the Book, that he came upon a toll gate at the entrance to a great highway, and there he beheld a marvelous carriage which dazzled his eyes. And in the carriage sat a man in strange garments with his head shorn.

DR. IVY: Hop in, Dad; want a lift to the city?

CHRISTIAN: What manner of words are these? And whither....

DR. IVY: Just sit down. I'm in a bit of a rush. What's the matter? Too fast? This Jag has a lot of soup. Where are you from? Destruction? Can't say I ever heard of it. Sounds like a good place to be from! What's the book you're carrying?

CHRISTIAN: Sir, this is the Book that leads me in the path of righteousness. Because of what I have read in it I am journeying to the City. Are you bound thither at this fearful rate, or is this the broad highway that leadeth to destruction?

DR. IVY: Not a bad term for this pike; it does lead the nation in traffic deaths. But don't be alarmed; I'll get you to the city. I'm glad you read the Bible, but isn't it a bit ostentatious to carry it in your hands that way? It suggests Fundamentalist bibliolatry.

CHRISTIAN: I know not who these are whom you scorn, but did not Moses bear the Words of God in his hand as he came down from the mount?

DR. IVY: To be sure, but you can scarcely conform your daily behaviour to the myths of heilsgeschichte, however meaningful they may be as witnesses to redemptive action. You don't follow me? After all, we know nothing about Moses. The Sinai tradition was Israel's way of historicizing the Babylonian New Year mythology. What is significant is the philosophy of history that arose in Israel in which Israel's past was related in mythological language to the act of God....

CHRISTIAN: But did not the King say, Moses wrote of me?

DR. IVY: No doubt Jesus accepted the traditions of his day as to the Mosaic authorship of the Pentateuch; but we must distinguish between the man Jesus and the Christ-event... DON'T OPEN THAT DOOR! I'm stopping!

33

Now I saw in my dream that Christian picked himself up from the ditch, and with great haste fled away from the highway, holding both his ears as he ran.

Championship Play

Now I saw in my dream, that as Christian toiled up a steep road in the evening, he came to a city set on a hill, and there was a great church there, and Christian quickened his weary pace to seek rest. As he entered a hall he met a man with shorn head.

DR. IVY: Good evening, friend. What a convincing costume! The stage lights are operating again. We've added another circuit. Will you be through with the play rehearsal in time to drop in on the bowling?

CHRISTIAN: But sir, I thought this was a house of worship — have I come again to Vanity Fair?

DR. IVY: I beg your pardon, I thought you were in the cast of *Dark Pilgrimage*. The sanctuary is open for meditation. This is the fellowship hall. Glad to have you watch the bowling, though. It's a match for the championship — the Men's Bible Class against the Usher's Association.

CHRISTIAN: A Bible class at the game of bowls? Do you thus redeem the time in evil days? And do you speak of stage plays in this place?

DR. IVY: You seem tense, friend. Perhaps we should talk this over. Here, step into our counseling room.

Now as I dreamed, I saw Christian enter a darkened room and lie upon a couch. Dr. Ivy began to converse concerning Christian's childhood, but Christian forthwith fell asleep. After a time Dr. Ivy left him. When Christian awakened he sought to leave, but hearing shouts, he entered a hall where men rejoiced at sport.

DR. IVY: There you are! The match is nearly over. This is the league champion about to roll. Has five consecutive strikes. Watch his follow-through! There it is! A strike!

CHRISTIAN: Would that such zeal were found among pilgrims to the celestial city! Alas, like Joash at the bed of Elisha, we smite but thrice when we should strike again and again till the victory is gained.

DR. IVY: The last one — a seventh strike! The ushers defeat the Men's Bible Class! What a victory!

Now in the tumult Christian slipped away and traveled on singing this song:

> When saints fellowship at bowling pins,
> Their mirth may cover many sins;
> But guttered are their life-score tallies
> Who seek the Kingdom first in alleys!

Old Grad

At our homecoming grid classic I was attracted to an Old Grad type who was blocking my view of the field. Several contacts were made during the game, mostly by his elbows, but I established rapport — after the winning touchdown — when he embraced me and then helped find my glasses under the stands.

When that old boy pulled off jersey 66 in '26 he lost not only his glory but his identity. Homecoming is the annual climax of his quest for community.

The pathetic Old Grad is a rare bird, but the species is plentiful in different plumage. There is the lodge member variant; in business men's clubs the cultic backslap is the mark of the order. The most ominous mutation has the widest distribution: the Old Grad Patriot. At a political rally he cheers the American Way of Life with the Old Grad's compulsive zeal. Secretly he yearns for a Big Game (with survivors, of course, to celebrate V-R day).

The Old Grad is an idolater. He seeks the meaning of life in communities which are only means in life. Loyalty to a group or a nation, made supreme, becomes a curse. Modern nationalism from the French Revolution to Hitler and Stalin has been a pseudo-religion feeding like a heavy-bellied vulture on the corpse of Christian faith.

We dare not offer the American eagle that diet. To insist in the name of democracy that a man's religious creed makes no difference if he is a "good American" is to make Americanism the only creed that is religious. Christ's disciple is a loyal citizen for conscience' sake, but he has one Master to Whom alone he renders that which is God's. Over all his loyalties is the cross he took up when he denied the world to follow Him. The citizen of heaven is not an "Old Grad" but a new creature!

Census

Pastor Peterson was deep in his armchair reading the telephone book. The church register was open beside him. He explained that he was preparing a sermon on Psalm 87. When I looked uncomfortably blank, he reminded me that this was the Psalm behind the hymn "Glorious things of thee are spoken, Zion, city of our God."

The census year had led him to reflect on the numbering of the people of God. Psalm 87 describes the glorious counting of the Gentiles among the citizens of Zion. At the moment, however, he was comparing the mainly Anglo-Saxon names of the church register with the cosmopolitan variety of the phone book. He had been scribbling the following verses.

I told the pastor that I rather preferred Newton's poetry on the psalm, but that I would look forward to the sermon.

O'Bannon, Shannon,
Maglioni, Gray, Brown
Are names now numbered
In the census count down.

Miss London, Naples,
Mr. Paris, France, Rome
Are all on record
In their U.S.A. home,

Along with others
Somewhat harder to spell,
Onuskanych and
Zyzniewski as well.

Each nose is counted
Every name is spelled out —
The Szuszczewiczes
Are inscribed without doubt.

The rolls of heaven
Must be stranger by far;
His book of mercy
Who has numbered each star

Is filled with names from
Most outlandish places,
The gathered harvest
Of the scattered races.

For Wu and Suki,
Mbuyong, O'Brien,
They too are reckoned
With the sons of Zion.

Hypertension

Do you find it essential
    to be existential
Since you've been up-ended in time?
Dialectical tension
    describes your suspension
For you dare not ignore Kier-
    kegaard's either/or nor
Expect to find reason or rhyme
In a life where the moment
    foments that sheer torment,
The crisis of being in time.

But before such deep pathos
  descends into bathos
And poetry drowns in a shriek,
I would venture to ask if
  this temporal casket,
Inner lined with red woes, is
  the cause of neurosis
Which we existentially seek?
As we trace all our crime to
  this framework of time, since
We're for the time-being too weak,

We are told that the blame must
  be ours just the same though
The fall did not happen in time.
By a timely invention
  we hold fast our tension.
Sharing Adam's declension
  outside this dimension
In new super-temporal time.
But in all this two-timing
  our ego is climbing...
Existence! So tragic-sublime!

Blaming time and existence,
  we keep at a distance
The guilt of primordial crime.
We are evil and covet,
  we sin and we love it
As did Adam before us;
  but Christ to restore us
Lived sinless in calendar time.
Both our fall and salvation
  took place in duration
In that frame of creation,
  that time of decision,
That daily and commonplace time...
Momentous significant time!

Fashion Guide

There is no better way to be different than to stay the same. Amish "plain dress" was once completely unobtrusive, but even Dior's latest is less bizarre on Fifth Avenue. Those cutting the patterns for the zig-zag changes of fashion have this worked out. Everyone, especially every woman, wants to be different. She can't bear to look like an ordinary woman. For every season she must find a new wardrobe that will flatter her individuality. Of course, she doesn't dream up a queer creation of her own. In fact, by studying the magazines, she has prepared herself for exactly what the better shops are offering.

This has to be different: the same difference for everybody who wants to be different. Now to make the different women different, style creators seldom think of anything new and different. In fact, this would be a waste of time when there is so much old and different. Therefore, the difference to which no truly different woman is indifferent is sometimes only different from the last difference, and may be the very difference by which women who are not different differ from the different! This Empire style, for example. Surely there must be a few recluses, in crumbling mansions or private institutions, who have never given it up.

The supreme act of courage is to stay with the difference after it is no longer different. Urge your wife to buy a sack at an absolute clearance, and wear it for three or four years. After all, aren't you still wearing those bargain pink shirts?

Unfortunately, style consciousness is not limited to the world of *haute couture*. Theological fashion seems equally potent, and appears to follow the same rick-rack pattern. Those weary of the new and different can be overcome with a fashionable rage for the old and different. Even a Neanderthal conservative is occasionally astonished at the authentic cut of the latest orlon bearskin.

The toughest assignment is to ignore fashion for the sake of truth. The theologian who seeks to build on the achievements of orthodox theologians of the last generation cannot boast even a modish bearskin. He must work in a pink shirt.

Cutting the Cloth

Pastoral Problem

Do you have a pastoral problem? Most church members do. Our forthcoming book, *The Problem Pastor*, has the latest patterns for cutting men of the cloth down to size.

"Group Therapy for the Pastor Who Thinks" is a practical chapter outlining a tested cure for the solitary cerebrate. He becomes addicted to social thinking and soon the bar of reason loses all its attraction for him. Small groups meeting each morning in the pastor's study continue the therapeutic process, since there is some danger of recurrence if he is left alone.

Is your pastor cordial and effusive? Continued use of our thesaurus of after-sermon comments will shrivel this expansiveness. Examples: "Have you had that sermon published, Doctor? It seemed so familiar..." "Thank you so much for that profound address. I never dreamed that text was such a puzzle!" After two months of this it will be enough to say, "I shall always remember the experience of hearing that sermon!"

Perhaps your pastor's problem is idleness. This often develops in those long days between Sundays when he has nothing to do. One contribution you can make is to help him with his reading. Choose a book at random from your late uncle's trunk in the attic and ask your pastor to read it carefully and give you his opinion of it. When he returns it, have two more ready. Vary the selection, using Watchtower publications, long modern novels (Is it *valid*, pastor?) and the *Congressional Record*.

If he pretends to be too busy, spend an afternoon at the parsonage in an informal check on his activities. Further spot checks may be made by phone or through friends. You may discover that his idleness is a mask; many problem pastors are frantic do-gooders, neglecting their families shamefully for parish and community activities.

Snap the tension of your strained pastoral relations by sending your problem or your pastor to us.

Pastoral Problem II

This interview is from the files of Pastor R., transcribed at the climax of his unusual career in counseling.

R. How do you see your problem, Herbert?

H. Well, to put all the cards on the table, pastor, I guess you're the problem.

R. I see. That's an interesting way to put it. Did your father frown on cards?

H. Yes, he did, but...

R. So to express a feeling of hostility toward me, you choose an expression that would offend your father. This transference of the father-image to the pastor is a common cause of negative affect toward the clergy. Do you have siblings?

H. What?... Oh. Sure. My brother Ray runs the Plaza Food Center where I'm a butcher. But what I came about...

R. You became a butcher after your brother was a successful store manager? How do you feel about your work?

H. Oh, I don't know. I like it in a way. Sometimes I think I should change to another job. But, pastor...

R. In other words, you enjoy cutting meat, but you also feel vaguely guilty about your job. Perhaps I can help you to recognize the character of the repressed feelings which lead to this ambivalent attitude. Resentment aroused by failure in sibling rivalry can find outlet in symbolic action. For example, you are no doubt unaware of that envelope in your hands which you have been creasing so vigorously.

H. Yes, pastor...I mean, no. Here!

R. Ah...it is from the board of deacons, I see. A request for my resignation, together with a number of rationalizations for this attitude. Did you observe a feeling of satisfaction when this action passed?

H. Some of the men were hugging each other.

R. Yes. Group therapy is decidedly necessary. Thank you, Herbert. When do you wish to call again?

Comparative Ecclesiastics

At the Women's Auxiliary Buffet, Pastor Weems, Dr. Ivy, and Dean Drinkwater were chatting as Weems finished a second slice of chocolate whipped cream cake. Studying the trio, I was reminded of the importance of Comparative Ecclesiastics, the psychosomatic study of atypical clergy. The following introductory descriptions are of value to research assistants, pulpit committees, and prospective ladies of the manse.

Ecclesiasticus Ectomorphus.

Solid supporter of church suppers, bake sales, teas. Often visits in the homes of his parish to encourage hospitality. A weighty opponent of asceticism. Prefers Genevan robe in pulpit (52, short). Jolly sermonettes a specialty.

Clericus Mesomorphus.

Enthusiastic keystone of young men's activities, notably at second base on the soft-ball team. Develops small group emphasis throughout the church year: bowling, basketball, tennis, golf in season. Muscular preaching with booming cross-nave volley. Casualties from handclasps at the door.

45

Doctorandus Endomorphus.

His immortal sermons never die, they just fade away. He carries the groceries with a scholarly stoop and drives his vintage Packard with philosophic detachment. He can sometimes recall the name of a parishioner by associating him with a Continental scholar.

Predicandus Amorphus.

All things to all men. An evangelical-liberal with leanings toward and away from neodoxy and paleoism. Heartily concurs in both sides of every argument — with minor reservations. Man of many deep convictions which last for days.

(Studies are in progress on *Tyranothesaurus Rex* who hurls synonyms like thunderbolts and defies you to break into his conversation, and *Dialecticus Non Dubitandum.*)

Pastor's Sermon Clinic

Many contemporary sermons are lacking in organization. Give your sermons the Connective Test. Listen to the tape of a recent discourse and check the number of times you have used the following:

1. And ... aa-a-a-a-
2. And, as We were saying ...
3. That, by the way, recalls an experience I had in ...
4. Or, as the Irishman said when ...
5. If I may return for a moment to the text ...

To score, divide the number of occurrences by the phrase number and multiply by the number of points, if any, in your sermon. If you have five or more instances of a phrase listed above, read the sentence below with the corresponding number:

1. You have a strong feeling for structure. Your hesitation shows a commendable desire to choose words having some relation to what has been said.

2. Splendid organizational unity. You remember what you have said, and repeatedly echo it. Symphonic mastery of a motif. (The We is the plural of a doctor of divinity.)

3. Deep thematic awareness. Each successive parenthesis ((properly introduced ((note the shared experience (((should be relevant ((((but not necessarily to the first theme)))))))))) leads to an existential denouement.

4. This brilliant extemporized connection introduces the Jocular Parallel, known to Hebraists as the Wow Consecutive.

5. A dangerous redundancy. Returning to the text will not only interrupt the chain of association in your remarks, it may also raise extraneous questions in the minds of any wakeful hearers: what was the text? what does it mean? why did he leave it? You can readily imagine the embarrassment this might become to your liberties in the pulpit!

If your low score reveals weak structure, use this outline for two months:

Theme: A Cheering Thought

1. Illustrations of Cheering Thoughts
   (Cheering Thoughts Cheer)
2. Illustrations of This Cheering Thought
   (This Cheering Thought Cheers)
3. Concluding Illustrations
   (How We Are Cheered!)

Various Cheering Thoughts must be supplied; at present we have none to offer.

Collage

Thanks to Picasso, collage is now regarded as a fine art as well as a kindergarten pastime. Recently a *New York Times* critic objected to the technique of a Swiss collagist who wadded up pasted paper to resemble oil paint. It reminded him of a woman who achieved newsreel recognition through the unusual occupation of making pictures from pellets of chewing gum.

Ecclesiastical collage is a deserving subject for thesis research. Comprehensive surveys of the undersides of pews would reveal collage creations accumulated by generations of discreet chewers. Chemical analysis of deposits might indicate when Wrigley displaced peppermints as sermon solace.

Pulpit collage is even more fascinating. Few pulpits have parked chewing gum undercoatings, but sermon collaging is a diligently practiced art. To understand the popularity of outlandish scissors-and-paste theories of biblical criticism, we need only to scan the sermon notes of the more gullible divines.

There are three main types of homiletical collage: the anecdotal, the quotational, and the sampler. The anecdotal is the most common and the most varied. It presents a sermon collage of stories, usually from the minister's own experience, real or imagined. The personality of the preacher determines whether the selection is humorous or lugubrious. Favorite classifications are: Personal Problems I Have Solved; My Summer Travels; Happy Memories of a Former Charge. A good anecdotal collage will not average above one minute of connective material between stories.

Quotational collages require either a wide acquaintance with literature or the Oxford *Dictionary of Quotations*. Long quotations from Shakespeare are favored; hymn quotations are excellent, particularly if the hymn has seven verses. This method has been falling into disuse, however, and is seldom found in churches with pew collages.

The sampler collage is a craftsmanlike assembly of paragraphs from various printed sermons that have some possible relation to the subject in hand. Fortunately there are manuals with material for this kind of thing. A firm artist's hand is necessary to hold the seams together.

There are many ways of expressing your appreciation of artful pulpit collage. Attempts at source criticism will show your alert interest. You may murmur, "Your sermon was simply mosaic! Wasn't that last issue of CHRISTIANITY TODAY stimulating?" Or you may whisper confidentially, "My cousin was a member of your church in Kankakee, and I was intrigued by your imaginative description of her neurosis."

Minister Cheevy

(With profound apologies to Edwin Arlington Robinson)

Minister Cheevy, man of cloth,
  Grew sleek while he assured the matrons.
He feared no wardrobe-eating moth
  For he had patrons.

Reverend Cheevy loved the sight
  Of crowded pews at Sunday service.
His rhetoric was at its height
  When he was nervous.

Pastor Cheevy could obtain
  Rapport with tense, neurotic people.
The soothing of his manner sane
  Was like a peace pill.

President Cheevy always ran
  Church meetings with a smooth decorum.
The board would somehow choose his plan
  In open forum.

Rotarian Cheevy could relax
  With all the boys at business lunches.
He knew the art of slapping backs
  And pulling punches.

Doctor Cheevy wrote a book
  That traced the road of human progress.
An author, father, husband, cook,
  He ran for Congress.

Minister Cheevy filled his roles
  With balanced poise beyond aspersion.
This guide of souls met all his goals
  — But lacked conversion!

Sacred Electronics

Now that the Jesuits use electronic brains for research, it is time for harassed pastors to discover automation.

Pastor Brown is already a short circuit rider. In his saddlebag for calls on ailing widows is a tape recording of Sunday's service. His simple visitation technique is to bring a table, find an extension cord, plug in the machine, replace a fuse, splice the tape, then nap with a suitably benign expression while his best oratory thunders at the widow.

One or two ministers of visual education, with suitable staffs, can keep the largest pastorate wired for sound.

For real automation such simplification of the ministry is but the beginning. By prompt action you may still sell your library before the conservatives realize we are in the post-literary age. Soon gleaming silver-green machines will line your study wall. Their quiet hum indicates they are receiving information by direct wire from the regional office, Commission for Group Therapy, Worship Division. From this your sermon will be accurately assembled and recorded (in your own voice — somewhat improved).

Even before this penultimate stage* immense benefits await you. Consider the efficiency of storing stock sermon illustrations on punched cards, to be automatically inserted on the tape where they apply! Think of the values of electronic committee meetings! Progressive pastors have already moderated meetings *in absentia* with a recorder wired to repeat the concluding statements of every speech in this setting: "In other words, you believe that... What reaction is there to this insight?"

A fully electronic committee meets in the machine. Deacon Jones' chronic opposition to the pastor, Elder Harper's allergy to doctrinal questions — all such factors are filed on tape, including, in Elder Biffle's case, the pronounced views of Mrs. Biffle. Anything can be decided in 47 seconds. The trained clergyman can adjust the machine to jam and ring an alarm when fed the question, "Should the pastor be asked to resign?"

*If you can't predict the *ultimate* stage, UNIVAC can!

Sermon Doodles

Dr. Knudal, one of our correspondents, received his degree in educational psychology for pioneering research in the repressed responses of a captive audience symbolized in sermon doodles. He has collected an initial sample of 64,926 doodles, representing the reactions of some 7,540 doodlers during 985 sermonic episodes. He plans to establish a clinic for the interpretation of doodles, and we submitted this sample for his comment. (The enumeration and notes are his.)

1. *Gesture motif.* One of the commonest preacher-based doodles. Significant index of character-image. Note mouth formation.

2. *Spider webs.* Intricate webs, coils, flourishes indicate impression of complexity. Check sermon structure.

3. *Traffic warnings.* Often sermon-orientated. Express resentment toward blocks in sermonic progress. 3? may be associated with this pattern, but is church location near grade crossing?

4. *Ecclesiastical architecture.* Usually suggested by church building. Visual exploration of interior is extensive and meticulous — fruitful doodle source.

5. *Flower table.* May be linked with 4 as interior scene, or with 6 below. Sometimes a doodle of contentment.

6. *Hat show.* In spite of association with 5, 6b is not an inverted flower pot. Hat contemplation unavoidable for shorter parishioners. See also Robert Burns, "To a Louse, on Seeing One on a Lady's Bonnet at Church."

7. *Time has run out.* Time-lapse doodlery common among sermon listeners. Smoke above 7b suggests fate of dinner in oven. Above smoke is hour glass (or coffee maker?).

8. *Neptune?* Rare, meaning uncertain. If sample is from the South, this may be a Yankee Doodle.

Suggestions

    a. Eliminate flowers, hats, architecture, etc.

    b. Eliminate pencils, visitor's cards, hymnal fly-leaves.

    c. Eliminate the preacher.

    d. Furnish each member with this essay and the doodle space below.

Preacher's Mathematics

From our *Preacher's Vademecum*
And Almanac for Clerics,
We bring this jingled guide to
Rhetorical numerics.
For every pulpit speaker
Must know the spell of number;
If arguments are weak, or
The nodding hearers slumber,
No study of linguistics,
Patristics, or the mystics,
Has half of one per cent of
The power of statistics.

Through mastery of digits,
Geometry, and Trig., yours
Must be the added duty
Of proving it with figures.
Percentages are potent,
And who can bring objection
To sociometric survey
With I.B.M. projection?
In analyzing factors,
No room for question lingers;
If you would make your points, sir,
Just count them on your fingers.
The graphs in paragraphs of
Your exponential preaching
Will plot a soaring orbit
Of influence far-reaching.

Yet numbers without nuance
Do little to incline us;
Your phrasing must assign them
A value, plus or minus.
A cold and empty zero
Is void if so you take it;
If vacuous, inane,
And uninformed you make it.

But verbal mathematics
Emotionally spoken
Creates a zero *plus,* all
Unprejudiced and open!

One minus — monolithic,
Undifferentiated,
Alone and solipsistic,
When differently stated
May lose the insularity
Of single isolation,
Becoming solidarity
In union with our nation.

"The schizophrenic splittings
Of deviating schism"
Are proper verbal fittings
For wicked dualism,
While twoness that we relish
Is favorably rated —
To praise togethernesses
Our verbs are conjugated.
If one is undecided
Which dual scheme to mention,
A polar dialectic
Will furnish both in tension.

        *   *   *   *

Rhetorical numerics
Adds benefits uncounted
But just be sure your numbers
Are colorfully mounted!

In and Out the Windows

Every preacher knows that illustrations in sermons are windows to let in the light. Some sermons are like railroad coaches, with windows regularly spaced throughout their length; others are ranch style, featuring one picture window. Homiletical architecture, taking its cue from contemporary building, is using more and more glass. Indeed, to change the figure, as every illustrator must, many sermons have so many windows and so little structure that they resemble not so much a greenhouse as a fish net, classically defined as a large number of holes tied together with string.

A window does not only function to admit light. Recall the experience of my namesake at Troas! (Let me here deny categorically that Eutychus fell asleep on the window sill because Paul's sermon lacked illustrations.) Many a bemused hearer has been lost from a sermon *via illustrationis,* that is, out the window. Consider the folly of the young preacher who on a June morning is the victim of his repressed desires and pictures an approach shot to the ninth green to illustrate his second point. The greater his finesse with his homiletical iron, the more squarely he will loft fifteen per cent of his hearers over to the wrong fairway for the rest of the service.

Illustrative windows have also been known to admit dust, bugs and noise. Red herrings have been dragged through some; others are service ports from which thousands of canned anecdotes slide down an endless belt.

One preacher's corrective is to compare illustrating to harness racing. That illustrative critter must be lean and fresh, it must move fast on the inside track, and most of all, it must be harnessed. Unless it carries the point down the homestretch, keep that horseflesh off the track.

Still better, board up those windows and distill a limpid prose like that of this letter, which is free of all illustrative additives.

Fellowship Quilt

In the bedroom at the old-fashioned home of the retired Reverend Van Dyke is a fellowship quilt of curious design. There are wheels within squares and spokes from the wheels. Or perhaps they are sun-bursts in window panes that spread across the four-poster bed.

Radiating from each center are the embroidered names of the pastor's flock. Here the ladies of the Dorcas circle are stitched in the rays of their square. Near the center are the names of the members of the senior choir in sectors of sopranos, altos, tenors and basses. In one corner is the male chorus. There are "memory" circles, and one center is labeled "Sunday School Class #7"; others bear the names of teachers.

A curious, but not a crazy quilt. I suppose it is a more constant comforter to the kindly Reverend than any electric blanket. The young Dr. Jones who succeeded him might not appreciate such a gift. It would hardly fit the contemporary decor of the new parsonage. Judging from the Doctor's encounter with the Martha Circle, he might find the quilt had some hot patches!

The emeritus pastor, being advanced in years, is rather sentimental. In his afternoon nap he has used the quilt as a prayer reminder. Sometimes he worked his way across so many squares that he quite forgot to doze off.

I'm not sure that such a quilt should be made for every pastor — there might be too many stitches and perhaps too much chatter in the making. Yet it would be splendid for every Christian to own one, covered with the names of the saints. Tucked under it on a chilly spring night, one might get to thinking of the Lamb's Book of Life and of the great fabric of the spiritual Temple in which we are wrought together, not as stitches, but as living stones, in the hands of the Builder of His church.

Sound the Trumpets

Thank you, sir, for returning my last MSS. with the rejection slip. Do you plan, then, to ignore the current discussion of theological education? Do you *want* ministers to have breakdowns?

If you reject my definitive work, you can at least reprint a classic on the subject: Cotton Mather's *Manuductio ad Ministerium* (Hancock, Boston), 1726. Only one title page and the preface are in Latin. You have a choice of two further titles: *Directions for a Candidate of the Ministry, Wherein,* etc., or *The Angels Preparing to Sound the Trumpets.*

Mather faces up to this mental health business right off. "In the FIRST Place, *My Son,* I advise you to consider yourself as a *Dying Person....*" Imagine "your *Breath* failing, your *throat* rattling, your *Eyes* with a dim Cloud...." Modern "candidates" will greet this abrupt introduction less with gasps than with guffaws. Yet as shock therapy in Christian realism it is worth ten hours of orientation courses anywhere. The tough-minded old Puritan was much at death-beds with the comfort of the risen Christ.

This Puritan realism about dying leads to a Puritan plea for living to God. Here Mather has the freshness of deep devotion. It is the quality of life, not its length, that makes it *living.* For the Puritan it was not a tragedy to burn out for God.

However, Mather does not encourage a martyr complex. He wishes his "son" a long life, and counsels him how to make the most of it.

He is never tedious. He admits that a Hebrew scholar is suspected of "being an Odd, Starv'd, Lank sort of a thing, who had lived only on *Hebrew Roots* all his Days," but testifies, "I scarce ever take an *Hebrew Bible* into my Hands, but I am gratefully surprized with something I never thought of...."

Read Mather on visiting friends, "foolish *amours,*" Greek accents, stolen sermons, and, above all, conversion. Theological education has much to regain before it can progress!

Spectators

Americans are all screened these days — by the TV set. The screen separates a few hyper-tense performers on a ball diamond or in the studio from spectators relaxing in the bars, living-rooms and dens of the fifty states. Never have so many lost so much to so few.

Fortunately some have escaped the contour chair of spectator sports. Even the country club has members who will occasionally desert the TV lounge for an afternoon on the links. As the coach has often reminded us, the school football program still demands self-discipline for the glory of Alma Mater and several thousand paid spectators. Progressive education has not affected squad scrimmages!

Off the athletic field, discipline is rare. Each fall school teachers face again the relaxed teens in loafers and desperately resume the struggle from a strategic position much deteriorated through the long summer truce.

A preacher can sympathize. The stifled yawns of relaxed worshipers are symptoms of spectator Christianity, slumped smugly in the sanctuary. The most evangelical parson might be tempted to prescribe for his flock the rigor of the canonical hours that summon monks to prayer.

Discipline should begin with the preacher. If he prays more in public than in private and makes fewer calls than any doctor, insurance salesman or Fuller Brush man, he needs self-examination. A popular style of preaching is the stream-of-consciousness method, a flexible, free-form discourse in which the preacher passionately or pompously says whatever comes into his head. The cure is the discipline of the study. Scientific exegesis of the Scriptures and a return to the bracing richness of the creeds can bring new meaning to preaching.

Lazy Christianity that avoids hard thinking and hard work will never reach America's spectators with the gospel.

Marking Times

Halloween Reformation

My forthcoming pamphlet, *Survival in a 'Trick or Treat' Raid*
concludes that Halloween is not only here to stay, but will enjoy
the same cancerous growth other American holidays have known.

First-aid is offered to stricken parents. Have you thought of sending your childen out early to ring doorbells, so that their accumulated loot may be used for your free distribution?

Another suggestion for your readers: Wrapping candy corn in
Gospel tracts can't be the best way to bring a Christian witness at
Halloween. Why not show old-fashioned Christian hospitality to
charm the hoboes, clowns, and other rubber-faced baboons that
appear for this junior shakedown?

Since writing this informative booklet I have been hearing more
about "Reformation Day." Apparently it was no accident that
Martin Luther nailed up his ninety-five theses on the eve of All
Saints' Day. The indulgences Luther was attacking went on sale
that day. Picture a priest posting anti-bingo placards on the eve of
the annual parish carnival! Perhaps if we took Reformation Day
more seriously we could awaken our neighbors from a misty rever-
ence for Halloween as a ritual of the American Way of Life to a
concern about the Gospel which is *The* Way of Life.

If Reformation Day only means staging successful rallies, however, the term should be used with apologies. Luther's sense of

timing was not that of an advertising executive but of a soldier. "Here I stand"... He challenged the lie with his life. His strong views are now discounted as products of his rude age. Modern ecclesiastical crusading moves in an atmosphere of sweetness and light. Martin Luther breathed the fire of love, which is quite different — love for deluded souls destroyed by a works religion, love for Jesus Christ in whose righteousness alone he was justified by grace. The Reformation was an onslaught of love on specific errors at the right time and place: The castle church door on All Saints' Eve.

Reformation Day

With just a bit of hesitation
I write requesting information;
I find that clergy of my station
Are asked to give an explanation
Of reasons for the Reformation.
I must confess in consternation,
Lacunae in my education
Create an awkward situation.
I've heard about predestination,
And even consubstantiation,
(And Henry's royal irritation
About a papal dispensation
Refused without consideration)
And Luther's themes for disputation
That promptly on their publication
Electrified the German nation.
But I must ask with trepidation,
If we may speak with commendation
In days of church consolidation
Of worthies of the Reformation
Who labored in indoctrination
Were negative in altercation
And horrified their generation
By the crime of separation?

— Eugene Ivy

Saints and Spooks

On the eve of All Saints' Day
The spooks and goblins play
And witches stir their brew;
For the balanced Middle Ages,
Before paying saints their wages,
Gave the devil his due.
This equitable spirit
Saved the treasury of merit
(Which no goblin or fey spirit
Could properly inherit)
While assuring the ghosts of a chance
For a lark in the dark and a dance.

We're well past Middle Age
But spooks are still the rage:
The kids are keen for Halloween
And now demand a Horrorland
(On Channel Z, color TV).
From these ghouls which unnerve us,
What saints will preserve us?
For saints today are quite passe,
We have only the stars made by movie czars.
We adore the gun-slingers
And the well-modeled singers,
But no star in Hollywood
Need be holy, pure, or good —
What all-star cluster
Could pass all saints' muster?

While a world without saints savors horror for fun
A weird witches' sabbath has fiercely begun
And horror in earnest closes its shroud
On the vacant heart of the man in the crowd.
Neither celibate monks nor the profligate stars
(Though the saints filled their cells as the drunks crowd the bars)
Could redeem or release from that spirit unclean,
The Power of darkness, the Prince Halloween.

Only the Lord of the age drawing near,
The Prince of Life, has broken the fear
Of death and the prison of sin,
Conquered the strong man and entered in.

"The Prince of Darkness grim,
    We tremble not for him;
His rage we can endure,
    For lo! his doom is sure,
One little word shall fell him."

So sings the ransomed sinner whose heart no longer faints
For all who wait Christ's coming are called to be His saints.
In hope they speak the gospel's word:
All saints' day is the day of the Lord!

Thanksgiving Farce

Pastor Peterson is down again with a severe reaction. He is allergic to American holidays. This time Thanksgiving has him in trouble. He was asked to prepare the pageant for the Harvest Home Festival, and all went well until Mrs. Patience Alden Strauss, chairwoman of the Festival Committee, saw the dress rehearsal.

The curtain parted on three Thanksgiving tableaux arranged across the stage: Pilgrims on the way to church; a picture window view of an American family at dinner; and the home team float in the parade to Mohawk Bowl for the Big Game.

The band played a medley of *Come, Ye Thankful People, Come; Hail, Hail, the Gang's All Here;* and *On, Wisconsin.* Mrs. Strauss thought that this completed the pageant and was applauding delightedly when the action started. The Pilgrims came alive, walked out of the woods, and gaped at the picture window.

A wonderfully confusing scene followed in which the Pilgrims gradually concluded that help should be found to seize this family of irreligious, bewitched heathen and commit them to stocks. The modern Americans had meanwhile decided that these Pilgrim actors were overdoing it, and directed them to the Mohawk Bowl parade, under threat of calling the police.

When the Pilgrims encountered the yelling Indians on the float, they bravely grouped for self-defense, and held their fire until the Mohawks made a hilarious charge with lifted tomahawks.

How the pageant was to have ended I don't know. One of the Pilgrims had put too much powder in Judge Ronson's old muzzle loader, and when it went off everything seemed to go up in smoke.

After Judy Trout had stopped screaming and someone brought aromatic spirits for Mrs. Strauss, Pastor Peterson tried to defend his satirical fantasy. Mrs. Strauss admitted that the awkwardness of having Pilgrim visitors on Thanksgiving had been cleverly suggested. She thought the dialogue witty in the dining room scene, and she especially approved Uncle George's speech explaining to the Pilgrims why an American Thanksgiving is above creeds and church-going. But she was offended by the implications of the "slapstick farce" that Thanksgiving has lost contact with the Pilgrim tradition. Her ancestors came on the Mayflower. Peterson cancelled the pageant but wished that every "Thanksgiving" farce could be called off — or transformed!

13 Shopping Days

Plunging into a parking space at the Grand Plaza shopping center, I brushed fenders with a faded sedan and recognized Pastor Peterson inside. He was waiting for his wife, and cleared the front seat of packages so that I could join him.

"Christmas shopping?"

He winced and suddenly thrust an envelope in my hand. In the growing dusk I read the penciled lines:

> *Hark, the tinsel fairies sing,*
> *Santa Claus will come to bring*
> *Lighted trees with presents piled,*
> *Rocket ships for every child.*
> *Gleeful all the space kids rise,*
> *Join the sputniks in the skies*
> *With the missile men exclaim,*
> *'Christmas sure was getting tame!'*

It was my turn to wince. Pastor Peterson not only admitted to writing it, but insisted that he was about to prepare a "realistic" Christmas program, including a litany to Santa Claus, and with Jingle Bells for an offertory.

Why was he so bitter? It began when his children wanted to miss the Thanksgiving service to see Santa arrive at the Plaza in a space satellite. He was further depressed by the mixture of syrupy "White Christmas" music and syncopated carols blaring from the Plaza audio system. Then he had passed a bargain table crowded with plastic figurines: Santa Claus, Bambi, Flower, Rudolf, the Holy Family, and a few shepherds.

"What good will it do to put Christ back into Christmas?" he demanded. "That's precisely the trouble. Christ is buried in Christmas. The nativity is only a Christmas fable, the least interesting one, since it is Santa who pays off. We need to get Christ out of Christmas. We need Christ to save us from our Christmas Christianity!"

The parking lot speakers boomed,
> "Veiled in flesh the Godhead see,
> Hail the Incarnate Deity..."

Perhaps somewhere in the crowd someone heard the words, Pastor!

Santa Forum

Our holiday feature is a forum in which leading spokesmen answer a question of absorbing current interest: *Is there a Santa Claus?*

PROFESSOR GRUNDGELEHRT writes:

Your question, unfortunately, is framed in speculative, ontological terms. I prefer to leave abstract metaphysics to the Middle Ages and to ask with contemporary, existential passion, *have we encountered the Santa-event?* The rich and diverse tradition of Santa Claus in its world-wide spread is a proper subject for historical and phenomenological investigation, but the real Santa occurrence to which it points lies beyond history in Northpolar Time, where all the relative longitudes of Greenwich time meet and are transcended. The descent of Santa down the chimney symbolizes the vertical relation of Polar Time (Schlittengeschichte) to standard time. As you participate in the stocking-hanging ceremony you await the Santa encounter in which he again becomes profoundly true.

Dr. Eugene Ivy says:
Of course there is a Santa Claus. Can you look into the sparkling upturned eyes of your little child as you hang up her stocking and not believe in Santa Claus? Santa is there, for there is real Santa faith. Scholars disagree about the historicity of Nicholas of Patara. Personally I believe he lived in Lycia in Asia Minor during the early fourth century, as tradition asserts. I am also willing to accept him as the patron saint of children, merchants, and thieves. The first of these roles is rarely questioned and the last two are increasingly vindicated in the Santalands of our great stores. But even if it could be shown that the Nicholas of history was unacquainted with reindeer, my faith in Santa Claus would be undisturbed. Aren't my children's stockings full on Christmas morning?

Senator B. B. Fuddle:
Yes, Santa Claus exists as the great unitive symbol of our age. Americans may be divided by creedal clauses, but they are united by Santa Clauses. Certainly Santa has an important place in our working faith, the American Way of Life. It is un-American to be anti-Santa. Fight de-santagration!

Mirth at Christmas

It is "the Season" again. Rudolf lights the way for many a fast buck, to the merry jingling of the cash register. From the money-changers of the Christmas Bazaar, indulging suburbia must buy junior's affection with bribes of magnificent extravagance.

Scrooge's Ghost of Christmas Future projected the old miser's end with dismal detail, but he had no inkling of his own prospects. The poor spirit has inherited Marlowe's chain of ledgers and cash boxes, lengthened by a century and the lead type of a million full page ads.

In part Dickens himself is to blame. Under the cellophane of our commercial Christmas is the lollipop of Dickensian sentimentality. Nostalgia for our lost childhood demands that we compensate for neglecting our children by spoiling them. We must have the same carols (whether they are incarnation hymns or folk songs doesn't matter), the same customs (enshrined in 'Twas the Night Before Christmas), and the same scenes (a "White Christmas"). Commercialism has only exploited our sentimentality.

But it is all shattered by a scream of horror. For an *old-fashioned Christmas* we must forget Hungary, North Korea, and China.

Yet on the first Christmas the Christ was born in a stable, and it was not long before the tyrant bathed all Bethlehem in blood to murder him. Jesus was the Man of Sorrows; his agony and death are not pitiable but awesome. "Weep not for me," he said, for he came to die and in death to triumph over sin and evil. Christianity is realistic. It has nothing to do with simpering sentiment. The joy of the herald angels abides in horror and triumphs in death. In the raging fires of our time the sentimental Christmas tree dissolves in flame. Only one tree is not consumed: that cross of Christ by which the redeemed are brought to the tree of life in the paradise of God.

New Year Bells

Dr. Samuel Jones of Second Church is eagerly anticipating the first stroke of the New Year. Over the traditional din of horns, whistles, shots and sirens will float the inaugural notes of the new Van Dyke Memorial Carillon in the church tower. The system is completely electronic, which in a way is a pity, but then bell ringing is an extinct art in exurbia. Jones himself has a romantic attachment to bells. He has replaced the manse doorbell with imported chimes so that each visitor is greeted with the conclusion of the 1812 Overture.

I imagine his dedicatory address on New Year's Eve will ring the changes on bells. No doubt he will recite Poe's poem in passing, allude to the bell ringing theme of his favorite mystery story (*The Nine Tailors*, by Dorothy Sayers), and recrack the Liberty Bell with resounding oratorical strokes. I just hope he doesn't lapse into Tennyson's "Ring out, wild bells" in conclusion.

We will all share his thrill when the midnight noise-making is overwhelmed by the majesty of the carillon. Bells are the voice of a former age, when the church spire marked the village, and there was solemn harmony even in the signal of alarm. This is the time of the siren, the shrieking howl of a maddened mechanical beast. Sirens on New Year's Eve chill us with prospect of atomic war, but bells speak of peace.

Yet even before the bells were the trumpets. The trump of God heralded the Lord's presence on Sinai, and the priests were to blow the trumpet of jubilee after the atonement in the fiftieth year. Our Lord declared the realization of the gospel jubilee in his own presence at the synagogue of Nazareth. The church needs trumpets and bells in the pulpit: the warning blast of impending judgment, when the trump of God shall sound; the joyful sound of eternal salvation in Christ's finished work. The trumpet of the gospel herald has the urgency of an air-raid siren and the harmony of choirs of angels, for it calls not just to a new year but to the new heaven and earth. The jubilee liberty proclaimed in the text on the Liberty Bell is the liberty of sons of God.

Valentine Bouquet

A rash of comic valentines has appeared at the Market Square Church. Results were unfortunate. These samples show the danger of such a practice:

FOR OUR PREACHER

I do not love thee, Dr. Fell,
The reason why I cannot tell,
But this I know, and know full well,
I get a headache when you yell.

S. S. TEACHER'S REPROOF

"Johnny Pistol, I declare
You've cut a curl from Annie's hair,
Carved initials in your chair,
And while I glared in your direction,

Put bubble gum in our collection!
If you don't stop, you shall not have your
Big gold star for best behavior!"

TO OUR ELECTRONIC ORGANIST

With calm deliberation
    you make your preparation
Depress the little stops...
    and Whoom! the detonation!
How can you keep your balance,
    serenity, and poise,
While stomping on the pedals
    that booming bass of noise?
Your grand fortisissimo piles
    the decibels in cubes;
What supersonic sock
    from the vacuum in tubes!
For a plaque above your organ
    we bring this metal casting.
We found it by the roadside;
    it says, *Beware of Blasting!*

THE USHERS

The marching file moves in style
    Down the aisle
In smooth formation. Each carnation
    As punctuation
Bobs as one. The offering done,
With crisp precision now retiring
And quite aloof from eyes admiring
They slip into a narthex pew
    Hid from view,
And there they shed the manner formal
Endure the sermon as is normal
With yawns and whispers, nods and giggles
Some gossip, titters, coughs and wiggles,
Each polished dandy munching candy.
This is the preacher's heart's desire —
To hush the ushers and the choir!

All Out for Easter

Pastor Peterson's Christmas peeve has carried over to Easter. He predicts that the Easter Bunny will soon be riding in Santa's sleigh. There is scarcely time now for the clearance sales in between. The pastor is depressd by Easter fashions in pew and pulpit — the liberal spending of the first and the liberal theology of the second. We are indebted to him for the following selections from his forthcoming anthology *All Out for Easter*.

FLOWERS IN THE PULPIT

The eloquent Doctor,
To the pulpit born
Wanders in the garden
On Easter morn

And, wreathing the garlands,
With poetic powers
He distils sweet odors
Of verbal flowers:

"Perfume everlasting
Wafts from springtime bloom" ...
Preaching in the garden
He missed the tomb!

Absorbed in the glory
Lilies may afford,
He beheld no angels
Or living Lord!

EASTER OBSERVANCE

To observe Easter season
Will cost her much —
For that mad little hat as
A lighter touch,
For the strange new dress which, as
Fashion decrees,
Must be quite free of shape, like
A French chemise.

71

Yet she bears like a saint the
   Financial strain;
She'll adorn Easter's pew if
   It doesn't rain!

MY EASTER

Easter is for everyone!
The Easter bunny brings
Baskets full of colored eggs,
And candy chicks and things;
Jelly beans and chocolate eggs,
My name in sugar white —
Must I eat my dinner now?
I just don't feel quite right.

Easter's not just eating, though;
It's so much more than that
Easter means that I dress up
In my new coat and hat
Daddy wears his new gray suit
And Mother her new pearls,
Handbag, hat, and dress, and gloves
And coat and furs (and curls!)

Easter is for more than that —
For music, church, and flowers,
Spring, and buds, and shining clouds,
And splashy April showers.
Easter comes so late this year,
So far past April Fool;
Best of all *this* Easter means
We'll soon be out of school!

*The above poem the pastor attributes to a school girl. He insists
that it was found in a seventh grade desk and that this establishes
its origin as firmly as any Dead Sea scroll.*

Flies or Ants?

Our patriotic picnic was over, the crowd had left for the lakefront and the ball diamond, and I remained, a sluggard among the ants. These regimented hymenoptera, with their proverbial industry, were transporting cake crumbs to their colony headquarters. My observations were interrupted as I drove away a fly which had buzzed up from a puddle of root beer to light on my nose.

John Ruskin once wrote a tribute to the fly as the freest, most republican (I suppose we should say, democratic) creature on earth. He contrasted the fly's impudent individualism with the instinctual slavery of the ant. Our bandstand orator of the afternoon had described communism as anthill collectivism. He too preferred the fly life.

I had supposed that Ruskin's dry admiration for the fly was an expression of nineteenth century individualism. He also observed once that no human being was ever so free as a fish. (Since fish can catch flies and flies fish, so that we have both flying fish and fly fishing, it is difficult to decide which is the better symbol.) It now appears that the fly should be cast in a symbolic role in this century also. What is more existential than a fly buzzing against a window pane? Perhaps the beatnik fly in a lamp globe!

Are we to choose, then, the liberty of the rebel fly, or the burden of the adjusted ant? As I swatted at the fly that had returned to my cheek, I decided for the ant. Anthill conformity is probably not at all confining for ants, and its efficient pattern is far more satisfying than droning meaninglessness.

Or is there a better candidate for Insect of the Century?

Pastor Peterson came back from the ball game with a sprained ankle and rescued me from my musings. He pointed out that it is not surprising to find all insect analogies to be one-sided caricatures of human life. True human freedom is the liberty of the sons of God. The real liberty tree grows beside the stream of grace from God's throne. Any view of liberty that ignores God becomes inhuman license or slavery; men live like ants or die like flies.

The Freedman

Emerson Johnson is forty-three,
  In the land of the brave
    and the home of the free.

Slumping at ease in his Rambler coupe,
  He is free on the road
    with no family group.

Thousands of fins line the traffic sea
  So his auto, immobile,
    of motion is free.

Emerson Johnson is free of zest
  Both his mind and his motor
    can idle at rest.

Dreams of his youth now have lost their fire
  And he sits like a buddha,
    without a desire;

Sits in the jam of the highway groove,
  As he waits in the heat
    for the traffic to move.

Free men must mark Independence Day;
  Mr. Johnson is free
    in an absolute way:

Free of the cares of financial strain,
  For his business is sold
    and no worries remain;

Free since the day he divorced his wife,
  He is loose from all ties
    but the bondage of life;

Free from his tensions and morbid dread;
  Psychotherapy failed
    but they opened his head,

Snipped a key nerve in his noble brow
  And so snapped his concern
    with the here and the now.

Who in the heat of that summer sky
  Is so free to relax
    on the Fourth of July?

Spending Vacation?

A life may be lived
And labor endured
In dreamy anticipation
Of days at the shore,
Of seafood galore,
And waves of cool relaxation.
A life may be lived
And labor endured,
But vacations can only be spent!

In concrete car courts
And motels of sorts,
These swarms of tourists unending
Are spending vacation
For their recreation,
Are spending, spending, and spending.
A life may be lived
And labor endured
But vacations can only be spent!

For planes and for cabs,
For restaurant tabs,
Or cruising smoothly by ship —
Each stop on the way
Has an invoice to pay —
In full, including the tip.
A life may be lived
And labor endured,
But vacations can only be spent!

To add to the thrills
Of running up bills,
The hosts and merchants en route
Have found a device
To soften the price
And flatter tourists to boot;
As life may be lived
And labor is paid,
So vacations may often be charged!

To get in the swing
Of this sort of thing,
Just plan a bigger vacation
And go where you would;
Your credit is good —
Installments shrink through inflation.
Your life may be hard,
But get a white card —
Then what a charge from vacation!

The moral is clear,
But why add it here?
(That fun-and-sun recreation
Just cannot be spurned.)
Yet *he is twice burned*
Whose shirt is lost on vacation!

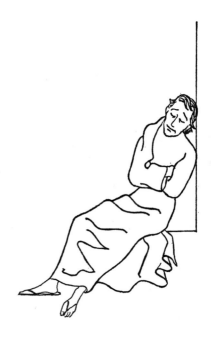

Teacher's Retreat

Limericks for Sunday School

There was a Beginner named Muntz
Who never missed Sunday School once;
   His award bars galore
   At last reached to the floor
From the stool where he sat as a dunce.

*   *   *

A teacher in primary grades
Loved audio-visual aids;
   She never was seen,
   For the filmstrips and screen
Required that she keep down the shades.

*   *   *

The committee conducted research
In the basement of Center Street church,
   And it silenced the noise
   Of the chairs and the boys
With carpet and switches of birch.

*   *   *

Librarian Lillian Gray
Read three Christian novels a day.
   When asked to explain,
   She replied with disdain,
"Don't you think I am earning my pay?"

79

Miss Fixture's been teaching for years
Countless classes of Primary dears,
  And now it appears
  That if she perseveres
Our whole staff will be leaving in tears.

*   *   *

Our class always meets to discuss
All the problems related to us.
  We can get most involved,
  Although nothing is solved
And we seldom remember the fuss.

Rally Day Acrostic

*Whatddaya mean, you
flunked out of Sunday
School?*

Some Sunday Schools have given up the time-honored custom of
having platform recitations on Rally Day, no doubt because the
teachers could not bear to hear the same old doggerel once more.
The acrostic below is from the new collection I have edited, *Rally
Day Revived*. The cartoon above is one of the many charming
illustrations which your own children may color during the program.

Remember, your neighbors
   expect it of you:
To send us to church
   is the least you can do.

Although we are little
   and somewhat naive,
We know every Sunday
   you sleep when we leave.

Long live our dear church school,
   for teacher is nice;
Her stories are sticky
   with pious advice.

Let's get to our sandpile,
   our crayons and cake;
When this thing is over
   we're off for the lake.

Yet, messing and glueing
   and learning by doing,
We share the great insight
   that makes us all one:
To quote our director,
   "Religion is fun!"

Zoo, Please!

James Younger, our new Minister of Christian Education, organized
our Sunday School pilgrimage to the Metropolitan zoo. Former zoo
outings were hectic and exhausting, punctuated with an occasional
lost child or lost lunch (before or after the picnic in the grove).
But this year Mr. Younger made the whole project a Planned
Learning Experience And Social Event (Project Zoo PLEASE).

After three staff conferences, a teacher workshop was set up to
discuss correlation with the Sunday School curriculum. Miss Fix-

ture refused to modify the lesson suggestions in her quarterly, but the others decided to prepare their children for shared experience in the zoo. Mr. Burns projected a series of Junior lessons on animals of the Bible: Eve and the serpent, Balaam and the ass, Samson and the lion, Elisha and the bears. No one else followed this lead, and it was found that a flexible lesson plan was important once the zoo trip was mentioned in class.

The Saturday morning departure time was delayed when an exuberant Junior let air out of the bus tires, but our two busses and small fleet of cars left well filled. Another slight delay resulted when one of the boys threw Patsy Miller's shoe out of a bus window. Fortunately, Mr. Younger was on the bus, and when the loss was discovered, it became a learning experience. The group decided that this was thoughtless behavior, and the bus returned to the Parkway where the loss occurred. Traffic patterns made it difficult to reconnoiter the spot, and when the bus reached the zoo an hour later, it was found that Miss Fixture had already retrieved the missing shoe, which had cracked her windshield.

For more spontaneous learning, the children were not lined up as before in touring the zoo, but were free to investigate in pairs of "buddies." This method developed many informal learning situations in encounters with zoo fauna and personnel. The zoo superintendent expressed to Mr. Younger appreciation of our visit and offered to provide a fully guided tour if our group should wish to come again after a year or two. He graciously furnished zoo guards to assist in reassembling the students when we were ready to go. The children had responded so actively to the project that it was after closing time before the last two were found in the moat around the elephant yard. The zoo chief himself saw us off with a pleasantry about turning his animals loose in our Sunday School.

Self-Service School?

Will Johnson came upon the test paper quite by accident. His eighth grader had left her stack of school books, gym equipment, notes, purse, and miscellaneous effects on the back seat of the car, and when he stopped suddenly to avoid crushing her bike in the driveway, the pile cascaded to the floor. The red pencil marks caught his eye as he was collecting the debris in a clothes basket.

The test covered a unit on personal adjustment. Pamela had not done well on it. Was it best to study: (a) on the floor in front of the TV, (b) on the kitchen table while mother prepared dinner, or (c) in a quiet place with good lighting. Incredibly, Pam had chosen (b).

What should a student do about a course he does not like? Pam had lettered briefly, "drop it."

Only one question received full credit. "What are your social needs?" Pam answered, "Acceptance, affection, achievement." Each was defined; achievement meant, "doing something better than others."

In the interview between father and daughter which soon followed, Pam explained that she had goofed deliberately. Writing the test, she said, had given her a wonderful sense of achievement. Even her teacher had overlooked the advantages of study in the kitchen, for example. What could better satisfy Pam's hunger for acceptance, affection, and a little food before dinner? It didn't interfere with achievement in anything but math, and a remarkable combination of low interest and low aptitude made it clear that math was not an area of achievement for Pam. Her advisor had admitted as much. Why should it interfere with her delightful kitchen adjustment?

Her father's response furnished Pam with a vigorous social experience of authoritarian parental control. She now studies in her room. At the PTA, Mr. Johnson's account of the incident led to spirited debate about the "social needs" approach to education. At the end, the discussion became theological, as Pastor Peterson urged self-sacrifice instead of self-service. He had seen too often what the quest for satisfaction of personal needs could do to marriages!

Have Fun!

"There is... little recognition of and reliance on the voluntary auspices under which the younger generation wishes to conduct its affairs, its insistence, to put the matter flatly, that work be fun."
—Sociologist at the Golden Anniversary White House Conference on Children and Youth, quoted in *Christianity Today*.

In conference at Washington
    An educationist observes,
Americans must have the fun
    That every grown up child deserves.

No sacrifice can be too great
    To subsidize our teaching staff:
We must learn how to re-create
    Our carefree, happy way of laugh.

In classroom frolic every day
    The droll instructor leads the way,
Or joins the party when it's gay,
    For all must learn that work is play.

And soon in shops and factories
    While music sounds and foremen sing,
The most reluctant boss agrees
    That in production play's the thing.

In government the men of fame
    Will find that paper work enthralls
When they can make it all a game
    And fill the file with paper dolls.

What morbid fear of missile-lags
    Can chill that patriotic son
Who bubbles with the latest gags?
    The nation's greeting is, "Have fun!"

But when this romping has begun,
    A single issue is at stake —
If all the job is really fun
    Then who will want a coffee-break?

Of course, you don't dig it, Ainslee, sermons are for grown-ups.

The E-Bomb

Pundits, statesmen and educators have commandeered the little moons as space platforms to lecture us about the scientific revolution. Survival now demands mindpower more than manpower. Only through education, say the educators, can we keep up with the Jonesevitches.

Publicity-minded pedagogues call it the E-bomb. It surely has a critical mass in our metropolitan schools. Is it clear how it helps to have the thing go off? Are the radio-active kids jiving in the new gym part of the fallout? The gang warlord who made his switchblade in the school shop is not well-educated, but would the E-bomb still be a dud if he learned to make a missile?

Even the "vision of greatness" as a neutral educational morality is not promising if the gang known as "The Egyptian Kings" happens to be most attracted to the greatness of Nero, Napoleon, or Nietzsche.

It is no solution, however, for evangelicals to throw rocks through the window walls of progressive education. Our stained glass windows are also vulnerable, especially those of abandoned churches in gangland. Courageous school teachers face young mobsters deserted by the churches in this flight to the suburbs.

A major breakthrough in Christian education is overdue: from the hour-a-week Sunday School (where no saint is more secure than Miss Fixture, whose practiced ineptitude has alienated generations of teen-agers) to a program of Christian nurture joining home and church in a curriculum to remove biblical illiteracy and train servants of Christ.

The Gospel once illumined all higher education in America. Another revival is needed — of Christian colleges, primary and secondary schools. The positive accomplishment of Christ-centered education can show the sweep and relevance of God's Word. We have a margin of luxury our fathers never knew. Do we have their vision? Even an atomic age cannot match the *dynamis* of Pentecost!

The Child and the Children

Dennis the Menace is a disconcerting American image of childhood. Our knowing guffaws at his pre-juvenile delinquency are in the same tradition that found Tom Sawyer hilarious. The novelist who pictured "momism" as the great threat to America must have had an unusual home life. The American home is not matriarchal or patriarchal; it is a filiarchy. We are not afraid of Big Brother. It is Little Brother with his six-guns who runs the ranch.

Child-centered living has at least made us more realistic about child nature. We may even be less inclined to adore the boy Jesus as a symbol of romantic, innocent childhood. Indeed, Christ Jesus was born of Mary not to symbolize childhood but to save it. Our hope is not in the children but in the Child.

Yet at the manger we learn not to despise the little ones. From Bethlehem, from the memory of Jesus blessing the children in His arms, flows Christian tenderness toward boys and girls. Martin Luther shows it. Beside the virile drum beat of "A Mighty Fortress" is the childlike simplicity of the "From Heaven on High" which Luther surely sang with his children and may have written for them:

Ah, dearest Jesus, holy Child,
Make thee a bed, soft, undefiled,
Within my heart, that it may be
A quiet chamber kept for thee.

Kierkegaard has "Climacus" say that Christianity is not for children. The reverse is true. It is for children and the childlike only. Jesus laid His hands on the children and said, "Of such is the kingdom of heaven." He is saying that to us of our children. In the Christ-centered home the child in the midst is not idolized but respected and loved, admonished and nurtured — in the Lord.

87

Ecclesian Made Easy

Lesson I

This is your first language lesson in Modern Ecclesian. (Dialectical Eglisais and Kirchendeutsch are available also.) You may supplement these exercises by attending selected churches and by reading journals written in Ecclesian.

1. TRANSLATE FROM THE ECCLESIAN:

a. By developing new perspectives in creative tension we shall gain fresh insights into the dialectic of our situation.

b. Our fundamental concern must be the existential expression of our solidarity in the ambiguity of the human condition.

c. Openness in history to the judgment upon history from beyond history when the historic becomes historical demands a meaningful encounter with mythological symbolization.

d. This is deep. This is big. This is man in his predicament. Today. Here. This is you. Now.

2. RENDER THESE IN SIMPLE ECCLESIAN:

a. I have a headache.

b. You can't get there from here.

c. Peace, it's unbearable!

d. Fairy-tales are really true.

3. VOCABULARY

Develop: to rarefy ambiguities in thought or discussion. Loan-word from Business English; used especially for committee reports.

Perspective: the horizontal structure from a given viewpoint. An invaluable term for reconciling contradictions. The plurality of perspectives is the structuring figure for unitive prose.

Dimension: see perspective. To give further perspective to all perspectives, add another dimension.

Insight, invaluable: the force of the prefix seems to be *without,* as in the term *income.*

The Human Condition: the mess we take pride in being in.

4. NOTES

a. Observe the shift in style in 1.d. above. This is Low Ecclesian. The staccato rhythm of this dialect gives it the relevance and immediacy of a dentist's drill.

b. To enter into competition for the Babel Medal in High Ecclesian, prepare a manuscript of fifty thousand words and send it to any reputable publisher.

Verdict in Ecclesian

The following selected passage is a supplementary exercise for advanced students. This remarkable document is the written verdict of a jury. The foreman happened to be an Ecclesiast with a strong background of committee work.

TRANSLATE FROM THE ECCLESIAN:

Our community experience of common obligation in the preparation of a verdict has been profoundly enriched by a stimulating diversity of viewpoint. The values of the course of action urged by the prosecution have been shared with us by several of our number, while the problems inhering in such a procedure have been called to our attention by other members of our group. An arid conceptualism of formulation would have most divisive consequences, even endangering the unanimity of our response. However, only the fullest facing of the issues can remove the schismatic, not to say fissiparous, potential of dormant misunderstandings. In the dynamic situation of this confrontal, we of the jury became gradually aware of the emergence of a totally new factor. We found that we were bound together in the context of a full engagement with respect to our differences, and this context provided a fresh setting for our common appraisal of these problems. This climate of opinion, this atmosphere of togetherness, has proved decisive in the attainment of full unanimity in the presentation of our verdict.

Since in his very innocence the defendant is guilty, and since we acknowledge our solidarity with him in this existential predicament, our verdict is that the defendant is guilty of innocence and therefore innocent of guilt. As implicated in this crime we recommend extreme clemency: sentence him, your honor, to life.

Humpty-Dumpty

Students of Ecclesian have access to many other fields of learning. The original source material which follows shows the value of a scholarly interpretation of a familiar text:

> *Humpty-Dumpty sat on a wall:*
> *Humpty-Dumpty had a great fall.*

We need not stop to discuss the critical questions which surround this classical text. It is generally understood by modern scholars to be a conflation of H and D. The Humptyist (H) may well have written, "Humpty sat on a wall." The original Deutero-Dumptyist (D²) probably had the reading, "Dumpty had a fall." A later redactor, acquainted with both traditions, and struck by the rhyming possibilities (Humpty/Dumpty; wall/fall) joined the conflicting accounts in a couplet. The adjective "great" is almost certainly a later gloss, which may be traced to lapsarian circles in Great Falls, Minnesota. The *formgeschichtlich* school traces the term to a *sitz-im-kindergarten* which favored exaggeration and legendary embellishment, but this has now been decisively rejected by I. E. Hohlkopfig (Z.A.G. XCMIII: 4, p. 116).

Our primary interest, however, is not in the vicissitudes of history which led to the challenging statement of the text. The fascinating speculations of Glowinkel linking our couplet with the festival of the Easter egg roll cannot be commented on here. We pass over the moralizing and allegorizing that many have found in C. Dodgson, *Through the Looking-Glass* (Ch. I, "Humpty-Dumpty").

Instead we turn to the simple declaration of the text. To be sure, the literal picture of an animate egg in a sitting posture on a stone wall is absurd from the scientific standpoint, for it escapes scientific categories. This fall did not occur in calendar time, but in the egg's act time, oval history. It gives mythological expression to the human predicament. As the Monarchist observes in those existential lines which he has had added in conclusion:

> *All the king's horses*
> *and all the king's men*
> *Couldn't put Humpty-Dumpty*
> *in his place again.*

Key to Ecclesian

Many readers will be vacationing in areas where High Ecclesian is spoken in metropolitan pulpits, and a brisk refresher will make it possible to distinguish the language from ecclesiastical Latin or political English (Ecclesian has much more affinity with the latter.) Earlier approaches to Ecclesian through rhythm analysis have been abandoned. Compare the following examples:

"The dynamic relevance of this climactic event, which illuminates by its essential brilliance the peaks and vales of history's horizon, burns also in your confrontation with the mystery of existence."

"You exist. Now. In the event. The world event. The you event."

These sentences mean roughly the same thing and provide some impression of the stylistic flexibility of Ecclesian. The sense in which Ecclesian is a tonal language is more debatable. Many masters of the tongue use decided falling inflections. Ecclesian has characteristic pronunciations of "static," "scholastic," and "creedal." The cultivated pronunciation of "factual" creates an image of a contemptible little brute, deplorably dense and useless.

Less gifted speakers, however, may also use Ecclesian. Its secret lies in the classic statement of Humpty Dumpty to Alice, "When I use a word, it means just what I choose it to mean—neither more nor less." Ecclesian impenetrability vanishes when Humpty Dumpty's principle is understood. (The learned egg-head defines impenetrability in that same passage, by the way.)

Occasionally a speaker of Ecclesian will say right out what he chooses to mean, which is appallingly bad form, but helps us get the hang of it. In a recent sermon the preacher chose to distinguish between "event" and "sheer event." Only the second actually happened, but the first is "true history." Can what didn't happen be true history? Certainly, because history provides the *meaning* of sheer events, and truth is expressed in fiction.

As Humpty said about his use of words, "The question is, which is to be the master—that's all."

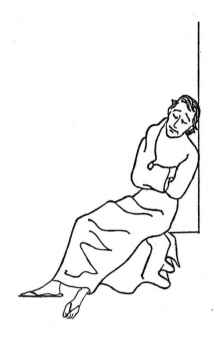

On the Shelf

Book of the Fortnight

This remarkable venture improves the best features of scores of book purchasing plans. More books are sent to fewer readers more often with less obligation. *You do nothing. Absolutely nothing.* No applications to fill out, no forms to return. If you do not wish to keep the books which you receive, give them away or throw them out. Under no circumstances are you obliged to read any of them. This ultimate plan is made possible by the generosity of a select group of authors who pay handsomely to have their works printed. Publishers are invited to participate with choice "surprise" stocks (trade term for works they are surprised to find still in stock.)

Book of the Fortnight offerings are reviewed here (although not all books here reviewed can be included in the plan). If you wish to become a member of the Fortnight Club, keep reading, and keep wishing. Perhaps your name will be chosen at the next centennial meeting of our board of directors. But remember, do not apply; you do absolutely nothing!

Our first offerings include:

Strange Stranger, by Ella Mae van Buiten.

A novel for heart burn. Glee Hopewell finds herself strangely drawn to this strangely forbidding stranger. Must she learn the secret of Agent 33? (Answer classified.)

Counseling Counselors, by an Anonymous Analyst.

The author was the prominent director of a famous Viennese clinic, who has recently been institutionalized. He writes from a first-hand knowledge of the field. In-service psychoanalysis is recommended through a new input-output tape recorder invented by the author.

The Committee Man, by the Committee on the Advancement of Ecclesiastical Committee Work.

This book represents the fruit of five years of committee investigation into the self-image of the committee man. It is composed of a symposium of self-portraits and a joint declaration which is useful as a master committee report for any occasion.

Dead Sea Treasure Guide, by Ali von Totenmeer.

Are the fabulous treasures described in the copper scroll of the Qumram Community still buried in Palestine? See for yourself with this do-it-yourself manual for the amateur archaeologist. Complete directions, Arabic dictionary, pick, shovel, etc.

KirKit, prepared by the Interchurch Service Consultants, Hybrid, Nebraska.

This amazing complete idea file has everything the busy pastor or church worker needs. Sermons, mid-week talks, dinner speeches are furnished in three forms: (1) manuscript, typed on three-ring notebook stock (with penciled annotations for authentic appearance), (2) outline notes, punched to fit loose-leaf Bible, (3) audio tape to be played on our new stereo-pillow system. No other service relieves you of *all* preparation. *KirKit* makes a master sermon part of you while you sleep! Also supplied: programs for the church year, menus for church suppers (our stocked freezer plan is extra), gala parties and hilarious ice-breakers, pastor's salary suggestions for the board of trustees, etc. Sparkling sermon titles do double duty as bulletin board aphorisms. Examples: "Whoever lives it up must live it down!"

Mgkykyii Returns, by S. S. Peters-Smith.

Mgkykyii, the mysterious witch doctor, appears again on the upper Congo. Can Nkrubezi and Mwawa find Bwana Schultz before jungle drums summon the tribes? If you can't guess the answer, this book is a must.

Inspirational Recipes, compiled by Manse Kitchens, Inc.

Intriguing, old-fashioned recipes are concealed in bright, sunshiny meditations. Hours of fun in discovering and testing the hidden formulas. For example: "From the lion's carcass of slain fears, dip a spoon of sweetness"=take one teaspoon of honey. Printed on indestructible miracle-foil; may be machine-washed or roasted.

Ghost Nations of the Bible, by J. Z. Obermacht.

A scholarly study of the fabulous peoples mentioned in the Old Testament. Like the "Rephaim" of the patriarchal narrative (the word means "shades"), these shadowy nations had no historical existence, concludes Dr. Obermacht. This edition is an unabridged reprint of the original translation from the German in 1868. Invaluable for O. T. criticism. (Dr. Obermacht's demonstration of the non-existence of the Hittites may require slight modification in view of excavation of Hattusas the Hittite capital, and the growth of modern Hittitology. Similarly, the Rephaim seem to be mentioned in administrative texts from Ugarit.) Librarians will welcome this definitive work, long out of print.

The Tweeter Twins in Dead Man's Gulch, by J. D. Wrangler.

To quote a comment from the sparkling dialogue of the Tweeters, "Ain't dis neat, Pete?" Peter and Skeeter Tweeter run out of gas in the historic dry gulch when they borrow a parked car to investigate the strange behavior of the ranch foreman. Thrills, chills, no frills, with an outstanding message (in bold-faced type). Drawings by a teenager. J. D. Wrangler is a leading juvenile author.

Summer Sleuths

In response to many requests that we provide *Book of the Fortnight Club* specials for summer reading, I have spent the last month perusing detective stories. This, I understand, is a leading variety of escape literature, although why anyone would choose this way out, I don't know. Real life must be frightful.

A student of the genre has concluded that the detective story is modern man's passion play. Evil is met and conquered — often by the brilliant reasoning of the "little gray cells," or by the omnipresent power of Scotland Yard. Sometimes sheer intuition shames the more methodical bloodhounds. More often, the emphasis is on the face-smashing vengeance of the private eye. The reader is supposed to identify himself with the gumshoe of his choice for a vicarious triumph.

Perhaps all this accounts for my difficulty in finding suitably edifying sleuths. No Pastor Brown has emerged to provide a Protestant peer for Chesterton's redoubtable priest. Of course the choice is narrowed a little by the *Fortnight Club* policy of distributing only author-subsidized editions absolutely free to those who do not request them.

The two selections reviewed below I finally wrote myself to exploit the need for summer diversion. At least two groups of readers can now identify themselves with a congenial Sherlock.

Murder at the Organ, by George S. Sanglant.

Sophisticated existential fiction. This is not a *whodunit,* but a *whydunit.* Inspector Migraine achieves such rapport with the criminal that the ambivalency of his motives becomes unequivocal. Migraine is easily the most non-judgmental detective in the business. The plot frays beautifully as he unravels it.

The Case of the Missing Xylophone, by Rex Stone.

Another first in Sunday School fiction; this paperback introduces Mike Angelo, chalk artist and amateur detective. When Patty Pond's xylophone disappears from the stage during the youth rally, suspicion points to magician Burt Berenski, an ex-convict. Who used the musical saw to cut a trap-door in the platform? Who recorded a talking horse on the background music tape?

Unless fellow readers can suggest an antidote I shall soon begin *Pastor Brown in London.*